MW00657604

OPERA JOURNEYS LIBRETTO SERIES

Giacomo Puccini's

LA BOHÈME

COMPLETE LIBRETTO
with Music Highlight examples

Edited by Burton D. Fisher
Principal lecturer, *Opera Journeys Lecture Series*

Opera Journeys Publishing™/ Boca Raton, Florida

WEB SITE: www.operajourneys.com E MAIL: operaj@bellsouth.net

Libretto

LA BOHÈME

ACT I

A garret. There is a large window through which the snow-covered roofs of Paris are seen. There is a a painter's easel with a half finished canvas, a stove, a table, a bed, four chairs, and books and manuscripts are strewn everywhere.
Rodolfo is thoughtful as he looks out the window. Marcello works at his painting, "The Crossing of the Red Sea," his hands stiff from the cold.
He tries in vain to warm them by blowing on them.

Marcello:
Questo "Mar Rosso" mi ammollisce e assidera
come se addosso mi piovesse in stille.
Pervendarmi affogo un Faraone.

Che fai?

Marcello: *(seated and continuing to paint).*
This "Red Sea" of mine makes me feel cold and numb
as if it were pouring over me.
In revenge, I'll drown a Pharaoh.
(To Rodolfo)
What are you doing?

Rodolfo:
Nei cieli bigi guardo fumar dai mille comignoli Parigi,

Rodolfo:
I'm looking at the grey skies of Paris where smoke comes from a thousand chimneys,

e penso quel poltone d'un vecchio
caminetta ingannatore che vive in ozio
come un gran signor!

Marcello:
Le sue redite oneste da un pezzo non
riceve.

Rodolfo:
Quelle sciocche foreste che fan sotto la
neve?

Marcello:
Rodolfo, io voglio dirti un mio pensier
profondo: ho un freddo cane.

Rodolfo:
Ed io, Marcel, non ti nascondo che non
credo al sudor della fronte.

Marcello:
Ho ghiacciate le dita quasi ancora le
tenessi immollate, giù in quella gran
ghiacciaia che è il cuore di Musetta.

Rodolfo:
L'amore è un caminetto che sciupa troppo.

Marcello:
...e in fretta!

Rodolfo:
...dove l'uomo è fascina...

Marcello:
...e la donna è l'alare.

Rodolfo:
...l'uno brucia in un soffio...

Marcello:
...e l'altra sta a guardare.

Rodolfo:
Ma intanto qui si gela!

and I'm thinking of that lazy old stove
that is idle and lives in leisure like a great
lord!

Marcello:
It's been a long time since he received his
just income.

Rodolfo:
What are those stupid forests doing, all
covered with snow?

Marcello:
Rodolfo, I want to tell you a profound
thought: I'm freezing cold.

Rodolfo:
As for me, Marcello, I'll be frank: I'm not
exactly sweating.

Marcello:
And my fingers are frozen as if I still
were holding them in that enormous
glacier: Musetta's heart.
(Marcello stops painting)

Rodolfo:
Love is a stove that consumes too much.

Marcello:
...and too fast!

Rodolfo:
...where the man is the fuel...

Marcello:
...and woman the spark . . .

Rodolfo:
...he burns in a moment...

Marcello:
...and she stands by watching!

Rodolfo:

Marcello:
..e si muore d'inedia!

Rodolfo:
Fuoco ci vuole!

Marcello:
Aspetta! Sacrifichiam la sedia!

Meanwhile, we're freezing in here!
Marcello:
...and dying from starvation!

Rodolfo:
We must have a fire!

Marcello: *(seizing a chair)*
Wait! We'll sacrifice the chair!

    Rodolfo stops Marcello. Suddenly Rodolfo has an idea and shouts with joy.

Rodolfo:
Eureka!

Rodolfo:
Eureka!
    Rodolfo runs to the table and grabs his voluminous script)

Marcello:
Trovasti?

Rodolfo:
Sì. Aguzza l'ingegno.
L'idea vampi in fiamma.

Marcello:
Bruciamo il "Mar Rosso"?

Marcello:
You've found it?

Rodolfo:
Yes. Sharpen your wits.
Let "thought" burst into flame.

Marcello: *(pointing to his painting)*
Shall we burn the " Red Sea"?

Rodolfo:
No. Puzza la tela dipinta.
Il mio dramma, l'ardente mio dramma ci
scaldi.

Marcello:
Vuoi leggerlo forse? Mi geli.

Rodolfo:
No, in cener la carta si sfaldi e l'estro
rivoli ai suoi cieli.
Al secol gran danno minaccia,
È Roma in periglio!

Marcello:
Gran cor!

Rodolfo:
A te l'atto primo!

Rodolfo:
No. Painted canvas smells.
My play, Let my ardent drama warm us.

Marcello:
Are you going to read it? I'll freeze.

Rodolfo:
No, the paper will become ash and genius
will soar back to its heaven.
A serious loss to the age.
And Rome is in danger!

Marcello:
What a noble heart! .

Rodolfo:

Marcello:
Qua.

Rodolfo:
Straccia.

Marcello:
Accendi.

Marcello:
Here, take the first act!

Marcello:
Here.

Rodolfo:
Tear it up.

Marcello:
Light it.

Rodolfo lights part of the manuscript and throws it into the fire. Then both draw their chairs close to the heat and savor its warmth.

Rodolfo e Marcello:
Che lieto baglior.

Rodolfo and Marcello:
What a happy glow!

The door opens and Colline enters, frozen and stamping his feet. He angrily throws some books on the table that are tied with a handkerchief.

Colline:
Già dell'Apocalisse appariscono i segni.
In giorno di Vigilia non si accettano
pegni!

Colline:
Signs of the Apocalypse begin to appear.
No pawning is allowed on Christmas Eve!

Colline interrupts himself, surprised to see the fire.

Una fiammata!

A fire!

Rodolfo:
Zitto, si dà il mio dramma.

Rodolfo:
Quiet, my play's being given.

Marcello:
...al fuoco.

Marcello:
... to the stove.

Colline:
Lo trove scintillante.

Colline:
I find it sparkling.

Rodolfo:
Vivo.

Rodolfo:
Brilliant.

Marcello:
Ma dura poco.

Marcello: *(as the fire diminishes)*
But it's a little brief.

Rodolfo:
La brevità gran pregio.

Rodolfo:
Brevity is a great asset.

Colline:
Autore, a me la sedia.

Colline:
Your chair, please, Mr. Author.

Marcello:
Questi intermezzi fan morir d' inedia.
Presto!

Marcello:
These intermissions kill you with boredom.
Get on with it!

Rodolfo:
Atto secondo.

Rodolfo: *(adding more of his play)*
Act two.

Marcello:
Non far sussurro.

Marcello:
Don't make a whisper.

Rodolfo rips off another part of the manuscript to kindle the fire.
Colline takes a chair and draws himself near to the fire.
Rodolfo stands nearby, ready with the remainder of his manuscript.

Colline:
Pensier profondo!

Colline:
What profound thoughts!

Marcello:
Giusto color!

Marcello:
How colorful!

Rodolfo:
In quell'azzurro guizzo languente sfuma
un'ardente scena d'amor.

Rodolfo:
In that dying blue flame there is an ardent
love-scene that is vanishing.

Colline:
Scoppietta un foglio.

Colline:
A page crackles.

Marcello:
Là c'eran baci!

Marcello:
Those were the kisses!

Rodolfo:
Tre atti or voglio d'un colpo udir.

Rodolfo:
I want to hear three acts at once.

Rodolfo throws the rest of the manuscript into the fire.

Colline:
Tal degli audaci l'idea s'integra.

Colline:
And your bold conception is so unified.

Tutti:
Bello in allegra vampa svanir.

All:
Joyous ideas vanish.

They applaud enthusiastically, but suddenly the flame dies.

Marcello:
Oh Dio! Già s'abbassa la fiamma.

Marcello:

Colline:
Che vano, che fragile dramma!

Marcello:
Già scricchiola, increspasi, muor!

Colline e Marcello:
Abbasso, abbasso l'autore!

Oh God! The flame is already dying.
Colline:
So vain, so fragile a drama!

Marcello:
It's already creaking and curling up to die!

Colline and Marcello:
Down with the author!

Two porters enter carrying food, bottles of wine, cigars, and a bundle of wood.
At the sound, the three men shout with joy, and fall upon the provisions.

Rodolfo:
Legna!

Marcello:
Sigari!

Colline:
Bordò!

Rodolfo:
Legna!

Marcello:
Bordò!

Tutti:
Le dovizie d'una fiera il destin ci destinò!

Rodolfo:
Wood!

Marcello:
Cigars!

Colline:
Bordeaux!

Rodolfo:
Firewood!

Marcello:
Bordeaux!

All:
Destiny provides us with a feast of plenty!

The porters leave. Schaunard, with an air of triumph, throws some coins on the floor.

Schaunard:
La Banca di Francia per voi si sbilancia.

Colline:
Raccatta, raccatta!

Marcello:
Son pezzi di latta!

Schaunard:
The Bank of France has gone broke just for you.

Colline: *(gathering up coins)*
Pick them up!

Marcello: *(incredulously)*

Schaunard:
Sei sordo? Sei lippo?
Quest'uomo chi è?

Rodolfo:
Luigi Filippo! M'inchino al mio Re!

Tutti:
Sta Luigi Filippo ai nostri piè!

They're made of tin!
Schaunard:
Are you deaf? Are you nearsighted?
Who is this man?

Rodolfo:
Louis Philippe! I bow to my king!

All: *(referring to coins on the floor)*
Louis Philippe is at our feet!

Schaunard tries to relate his good fortune, but the others are heedless, all busily placing the provisions on the table and the firewood in the stove.

Schaundard:
Or vi dirò: quest'oro, o meglio, argento,
ha la sua brava istoria.

Rodolfo:
Riscaldiamo il camino!

Colline:
Tanto freddo ha sofferto!

Schaunard:
Un inglese, un signor, lord o milord
che sia volea un musicista.

Marcello:
Via! Prepariamo la tavola!

Schaunard:
Io? Volo!

Rodolfo:
L'esca dov'è?

Colline:
Là!

Marcello:
Qua.

Schaunard:
E mi presento. M'accetta, gli domando.

Colline:
Arrosto freddo!

Schaunard:
Now I'll tell you: this gold, or better, this
silver, has a noble history.

Rodolfo:
Let's warm up the stove!

Colline:
It has suffered so much in this cold!

Schaunard:
An Englishman, a gentleman, a lord was
looking for a musician.

Marcello:
Go away! Let's set the table!

Schaunard:
And I? I flew to him.

Rodolfo:
Where are the matches?

Colline:
There!

Marcello:
Here.

Schaunard:
I introduce myself. He hires me, I ask him.

Colline:

Marcello:
Pasticcio dolce!

Schaunard:
A quando le lezioni?
Risponde:" Incominciam! Guardare!"
e un pappagallo m'addita al primo pian,
poi soggiunge:
"Voi suonare finchè quello morire!"

Rodolfo:
Fulgida folgori la sala splendida!

Marcello:
Ora le candele!

Schaunard:
E fu così:
suonai tre lunghi dì.
Allora usai l'incanto di mia presenza
bella. Affascinai l'ancella.
Gli propinai prezzemolo!
Lorito allargò l'ali,
Lorito il becco aprì,
da Socrate morìi!

Colline:
Pasticcio dolce!

Marcello:
Mangiar senza tovaglia?

Rodolfo:
No: un'idea!

Marcello e Colline:
II "Costituzional!"

Rodolfo:
Ottima carta.
Si mangia a si divora un'appendice!

Colline:
Chi?

Cold roast beef!
Marcello:
Sweet pastry!

Schaunard:
When do the lessons begin?
He replies: "Let's start! Look!"
and he points to a parrot on the first floor,
and then adds:
"You play until that bird dies!"

Rodolfo
The dining room's brilliant!

Marcello:
Now the candles!

Schaunard:
And so it went:
I played for three long days.
Then I used my charm, my handsome
figure, I won over the serving-girl.
We gave a little parsley to the parrot!.
Polly spread its wings,
Polly opened its beak, took a piece of
parsley, and died like Socrates!

Colline:
Sweet pastry!

Marcello:
Eating without a tablecloth?

Rodolfo: *(Rodolfo takes a newspaper)*
No! I've an idea.

Marcello and Colline:
The "Constitutional"!

Rodolfo:
Excellent paper.
You eat and devour a supplement!

Colline: *(to Schaunard)*
Who?

Schaunard:
Il diavolo vi porti tutti quanti!
Ed or che fate?
No! queste cibarie sono la salmeria pei dì
futuri tenebrosi e oscuri.
Pranzare in casa il dì della Vigilia mentre
il Quartier Latino le sue vie
addobba di salsiccie e leccornie?
Quando un olezzo di fritelle imbalsama le
vecchie strade? Là le ragazze cantano
contente.

.

Tutti:
La vigilia di Natal!

Schaunard:
Ed han per eco, ognuna uno studente!
Un po' di religione, o miei signori: si
beva in casa, ma si pranzi fuor.

Schaunard:
Go to the devil, all of you . . .
Now what are you doing?
No! These delicacies are the provisions for
dark and gloomy days in the future. Dine at
home on Christmas Eve when the Latin
Quarter has decked its streets with food?
When the perfume of fritters is wafted
through the ancient streets?
There the girls sing happily.

All:
It's Christmas Eve!

Schaunard
And each has a student echoing her!
Have some religion, gentlemen: we drink
at home, but we dine out.

As they pour wine there is a knock at the door.

Benoit:
Si può?

Benoit: *(from outside)*
May I come in?

Marcello:
Chi è là?

Marcello:
Who's there?

Benoit:
Benoit.

Benoit:
Benoit.

Marcello:
Il padrone di casa!

Marcello:
The landlord!

Schaunard:
Uscio sul muso.

Schaunard:
Bolt the door.

Colline:
Non c'è nessuno.

Colline:
Nobody's home.

Schaunard:
E chiuso.

Schaunard:
It's locked.

Benoit:
Una parola.

Benoit:
Just one word.

Schaunard:
Sola!

Benoit:
Affitto.

Marcello:
Olà. Date una sedia.

Rodolfo:
Presto.

Benoit:
Non occorre, io vorrei . . .

Schaunard:
Segga.

Marcello:
Vuol bere?

Benoit:
Grazie.

Rodolfo e Colline:
Tocchiamo.

Schaunard:
Beva.

Schaunard: *(opens the door)*
Just one!

(Benoit enters and shows a paper.)
Benoit:
Rent.

Marcello:
Here! Give him a chair.

Rodolfo:
Quickly.

Benoit:
Don't bother, I'd like . . .

Schaunard:
Be seated.

Marcello:
Something to drink?

Benoit:
Thank you.

Rodolfo and Colline:
A toast.

Schaunard:
Drink.

Benoit sets down his glass and shows the paper to Marcello.

Benoit:
Questo è l'ultimo trimestre.

Benoit:
This is the bill for three month's rent.

Marcello:
E n'ho piacere.

Marcello:
That's fine.

Benoit:
E quindi.

Benoit:
Therefore.

Schaunard:
Ancora un sorso.

Schaunard:
Another drop.

Benoit:
Grazie.

Benoit:
Thank you.

I Quattro:
Tocchiam.

The Four:
Let's drink.

Benoit:
Grazie.

Benoit:
Thanks.

I Quattro:
Alla sua salute!

The Four:
To your health!

Benoit:
A lei ne vengo perchè il trimestre scorso mi promise.

Benoit: *(to Marcello again)*
I come to you because last quarter you promised me.

Marcello:
Promisi ed or mantengo.

Marcello:
I promised and I'll pay.
(He points to the money on the table.)

Rodolfo:
Che fai?

Rodolfo: *(aside to Marcello)*
What are you doing?

Schaunard:
Sei pazzo?

Schaunard:
Are you crazy?

Marcello:

Ha visto? Or via, resti un momento in nostra compagnia.
Dica: quant'anni ha, caro Signor Benoit?

Marcello:
(to Benoit, ignoring the others)
You see? Don't go.
Stay with us a moment.
Tell me: how old are you, dear M. Benoit?

Benoit:
Gli anni? Per carità!

Benoit:
My age? Spare me!

Rodolfo:
Su a giù la nostra età.

Rodolfo:
Your age, more or less.

Benoit:
Di più, molto di più.

Benoit:
More, much more.

While they chat, they refill Benoit's empty glass.

Colline:
Ha detto su a giù.

Colline
He said more or less.

Marcello:
L'altra sera al Mabil l'han colto in peccato d'amor.

Marcello
The other evening at the Mabille they caught him making sinful love.

Benoit:
Io?

Benoit:
Me?

Marcello:
Al Mabil l'altra sera l'han colto.
Neghi?

Marcello:
They caught you at the Mabille the other
evening. Do you deny it?

Benoit:
Un caso.

Benoit:
An accident.

Marcello:
Bella donna!

Marcello:
A lovely woman!

Benoit:
Ah! molto!

Benoit: *(half drunk)*
Ah! Too much!

Schaunard poi Rodolfo:
Briccone!

Schaunard then Rodolfo:
You rascal!

Colline:
Seduttore! Una quercia . . . un cannone!

Colline:
Seducer! He's an oak, a ball of fire!

Rodolfo:
L'uomo ha buon gusto.

Rodolfo:
He's a man of taste.

Marcello:
Il crin ricciuto e fulvo.
Ei gongolava arzillo e pettoruto.

Marcello:
With that curly, tawny hair.
How he swaggered, proud and happy!

Benoit:
Son vecchio ma robusto.

Benoit:
I'm old but robust.

Colline, Schaunard, e Rodolfo:
Ei gongolava arzuto e pettorilio.

Colline, Schaunard, and Rodolfo:
How he swaggered, proud and happy!

Marcello:
E a lui cedea la femminil virtù.

Marcello:
Feminine virtue gave in to him.

Benoit:
Timido in gioventù, ora me ne ripago.
Si sa, è uno svago qualche donnetta
allegra . . . e . . . un po'.Non dico una
balena o un mappamondo, o un viso
tondo da luna piena.Ma magra, proprio
magra, no, poi no! Le donne magre son
grattacapi e spesso, sopracapi, e son piene
di doglie, per esempio,mia moglie . . .

Benoit:
I'm avenging my youthful timidity.
You know, a lovely woman is my hobby .
....a bit .I don't mean like a whale or a
map of the world or a face like a full
moon. But thin, really thin. No!
Thin women are worrisome and often . . .
a nuisance always full of complaints,
for example my wife . . .

Marcello rises, feigning moral indignation. The others do the same.

Marcello:
Quest'uomo ha moglie e sconcie voglie
ha nel cor!

Marcello:
This man has a wife and hides evil desires
in his heart!

Gli Altri:
Orror!

The Others:
Horror!

Rodolfo:
E ammorba, a appesta la nostra onesta
magion.

Rodolfo:
He corrupts and pollutes our respectable
home.

Gli Altri:
Fuor!

Others:
Out with him!

Marcello:
Si abbruci dello zucchero!

Marcello:
Burn some incense!

Colline:
Si discacci il reprobo.

Colline:
Throw out the scoundrel!

Schaunard:
È la morale offesa che vi scaccia!

Schaunard:
Our offended morality expels you!

Benoit:
Io di . . . io di . . .

Benoit:
I said . . . I . . .

Gli Altri:
Silenzio!

The Others:
Silence!

Benoit:
Miei signori . . .

Benoit:
My dear sirs . . .

Gli Altri:
Silenzio . . . via signore . . .
Via di qua!
E buona sera a vostra signoria!
Ah! Ah! Ah!

The Others:
Silence . . . out, sir . . .
Away with you!
And good evening to your lady!
Ha! Ha! Ha!

(Benoit is thrown out.)

Marcello:
Ho pagato il trimestre.

Marcello:
I've paid the rent.

Schaunard:
Al Quartiere Latin ci attende Momus.

Schaunard:
To the Latin Quarter where Momus awaits us.

Marcello:
Viva chi spende!

Marcello:
Long life to him who pays!

Schaunard:
Dividiamo il bottin!

Schaunard:
We'll divide my loot!

Gli Altri:
Dividiam!

The Others:
Let's divide!

(They share the coins.)

Marcello:
Là ci son beltà scese dal cielo.
Or che sei ricco, bada alla decenza!
Orso, ravviati il pelo.

Marcello: *(giving Colline a mirror)*
There are heavenly beauties there.
Now that you're rich, you must look
presentable. You bear! Trim your fur.

Colline:
Farò la conoscenza la prima volta d'un
barbitonsore. Guidatemi al ridicolo
oltraggio d'un rasoio.

Colline:
I'll make my first acquaintance with a
beard-barber. Lead me to the absurd,
outrageous razor.

Tutti:
Andiam.

All:
Let's go.

Rodolfo:
Io resto per terminar l'articolo di fondo
del Castoro.

Rodolfo:
I must stay to finish my article for the
Beaver.

Marcello:
Fa presto.

Marcello:
Do it fast!

Rodolfo:
Cinque minuti. Conosco il mestier.

Rodolfo:
Five minutes. I know my trade.

Colline:
T'aspetterem dabbasso dal portier.

Colline:
We'll wait for you downstairs.

Marcello:
Se tardi udrai the coro.

Marcello:
You'll hear us if you're late.

Rodolfo:
Cinque minuti.

Rodolfo:
Five minutes.

Schaunard:
Taglia corta la coda al tuo Castoro.

Schaunard:
Cut that Beaver's tail short.

(

Rodolfo takes the light and opens the door. The others start down the stairs.

Marcello:
Occhio alla scala. Tieni alla ringhiera.

Marcello: *(from the stairs)*
Watch the stairs. Hold on to the railing.

Rodolfo:
Adagio.

Rodolfo: *(raising the light)*
Go slowly.

Colline:
E buio pesto.

Colline:
It's pitch dark.

Schaunard:
Maledetto portier!

Schaunard:
That damn janitor!

Colline:
Accidenti!

Colline:
An accident!

Rodolfo:
Colline, sei morto?

Rodolfo:
Colline, are you dead?

Colline:
Non ancor.

Colline: *(from below)*
Not yet.

Marcello:
Vien presto.

Marcello:
Come soon.

Rodolfo closes the door, sets his light on the table and tries to write.
Uninspired, he tears up the paper and throws the pen down.

Rodolfo:
Non sono in vena.

Chi è là?

Rodolfo:
I'm not inspired.
(There's a timid knock at the door.)
Who's there?

Mimi:
Scusi.

Mimi: *(outside)*
Excuse me.

Rodolfo:
Una donna!

Rodolfo:
A woman!

Mimi:
Di grazia, mi si è spento il lume.

Mimi:
I'm sorry . . . my light has gone out.

Rodolfo:
Ecco.

Rodolfo: *(opening the door)*
Here.

Mimi:

Vorrebbe . . . ?

Rodolfo:
S'accomodi un momento.

Mimi:
Non occorre.

Rodolfo:
La prego, entri.

Si sente male?

Mimi:
No . . . nulla.

Rodolfo:
Impallidisce!

Mimi:
È il respir . . . quelle scale . . .

Mimi:
(appears in the doorway holding the spent candle in her hand and a key)
Would you . . . ?

Rodolfo:
Make yourself comfortable for a moment.

Mimi:
That's not necessary.

Rodolfo:
Please . . . come in.
(Mimi enters, and has a fit of coughing.)
You're not well?

Mimi:
No . . . it's nothing.

Rodolfo:
You're pale!

Mimi
I'm out of breath . . . the stairs . . .

Mimi faints, and Rodolfo catches her and helps her to a chair.
The key and the candlestick fall from her hands.

Rodolfo:
Ed ora come faccio?

Cosi. Che viso d'ammalata!

Si sente meglio?

Rodolfo:
Now what shall I do?
(He gets some water and sprinkles her face.)
So. How sickly she looks!

(Mimi revives.)
Are you better now?

Mimi
Sì.

Mimi:
Yes.

Rodolfo:
Qui c'è tanto freddo. Segga vicino al fuoco.

Aspetti . . . un po' di vino.

Rodolfo:
It's so cold here. Come and sit by the fire.

(He helps her to a chair by the stove.)
Wait . . . some wine.

Mimi:
Grazie.

Rodolfo:
A lei.

Mimi:
Poco, poco.

Rodolfo:
Così.

Mimi:
Grazie.

Rodolfo:
(Che bella bambina!)

Mimi:
Ora permetta che accenda il lume.
Tutto è passato.

Rodolfo:
Tanta fretta!

Mimi:
Sì.

Grazie. Buona sera.

Rodolfo:
Buona sera.

Mimi:
Oh! sventata, sventata!
la chiave della stanza dove l'ho lasciata?

Rodolfo:
Non stia sull'uscio: il lume vacilla al
vento.

Mimi:
Oh Dio! Torni ad accenderlo.

Mimi:
Thank you.

Rodolfo:
Here.

Mimi:
Just a little.

Rodolfo:
There.

Mimi:
Thank you.

Rodolfo:
(What a beautiful young girl!)

Mimi: *(rising)*
Now, please, relight my candle.
I'm better now.

Rodolfo:
Why such a hurry!

Mimi:
Yes.
(Rodolfo lights her candle.)
Thank you. Good evening.

Rodolfo:
Good evening.

(Mimi leaves, but then reappears at the door.)

Mimi:
Oh! Foolish me!
Where have I left the key to my room?

Rodolfo:
Don't stand at the door: the wind makes
your light flicker.
(Her candle goes out.)

Mimi:
Heavens! Will you relight it?

Rodolfo runs to her with his light, but when he reaches the door,
his candle also goes out. The room is dark.

Rodlfo:
Oh Dio! Anche il mio s'è spento.

Mimi:
Ah! E la chiave ove sarà?

Rodolfo:
Buio pesto!

Mimi:
Disgraziata!

Rodolfo:
Ove sarà?

Mimi:
Importuna è la vicina . . .

Rodolfo:
Ma le pare!

Mimi:
Importuna è la vicina . . .

Rodolfo:
Cosa dice? ma le pare!

Mimi:
Cerchi.

Rodolfo:
Cerco.

Mimi:
Ove sarà?

Rodolfo:
Ah!

Mimi:
L'ha trovata?

Rodolfo:
There . . . Now mine's out, too.

Mimi:
Ah! And where can my key be?

Rodolfo:
Pitch dark!

Mimi:
Unlucky me!

Rodolfo:
Where can it be?

Mimi:
You've an unfortunate neighbor . . .

Rodolfo:
Not at all.

Mimi:
You've an unfortunate neighbor . . .

Rodolfo:
What do you mean? Not at all!

Mimi:
Search for it.

Rodolfo:
I'm searching.

(They search, touching the floor with their hands.)

Mimi:
Where can it be?

Rodolfo:
Ah!
(He finds the key and puts it in his pocket.)

Mimi:
Did you find it?

Rodolfo:
No.

Rodolfo:
No.

Mimi:
Mi parve . . .

Mimi:
I thought . . .

Rodolfo:
In verità!

Rodolfo:
Truthfully!

Mimi:
Cerca?

Mimi:
Are you searching?

Rodolfo:
Cerco.

Rodolfo:
I'm searching for it.

*Guided by her voice, Rodolfo pretends to search as he draws closer to her.
Then he grasps her hand.*

Mimi:
Ah!

Mimi: *(surprised)*
Ah!

Andantino affetuoso
RODOLFO

Che ge - li - da ma - ni - na, se la la-sci ris -cal - dar,

Rodolfo:
Che gelida manina!
Se la lasci riscaldar.
Cercar che giova? Al buio non si trova.
Ma per fortuna è una notte di luna,
e qui la luna l'abbiamo vicina.
Aspetti, signorina, le dirò con due parole
chi son, chi son, e che faccio, come vivo.
Vuole?
Chi son? Chi son? Son un poeta.
Che cosa faccio? Scrivo.
E come vivo? Vivo.
In povertà mia lieta scialo da gran signore
rime ed inni d'amore.
Per sogni a per chimere e per castelli in
aria l'anima ho milionaria.

Rodolfo:
How cold your little hand is!
Let me warm it for you.
What's the use of searching? We'll never
find it in the dark. But luckily there's a
moon, and she's our neighbor here.
Just wait, my dear young lady, and
meanwhile I'll tell you in two words who
I am, what I do, and how I live. Shall I?
Who am I? Who am I? I'm a poet.
What do I do? I write.
How do I live? I live.
In my happy poverty I scale to heaven
with my poems and songs of love.
I'm a millionaire in spirit, with hopes,
dreams, and heavenly castles.

Con molto espressione
RODOLFO

Ta -lor dal mio for - zi - e - re,   ruban tutti i gioelli due ladri gli occhi belli.

Talor dal mio forziere ruban tutti i gioielli
due ladri: gli occhi belli.
V'entrar con voi pur ora ed i miei sogni
usati, ed i bei sogni miei tosto si dileguar!
Ma il furto non m'accora poichè, poichè
v'ha preso stanza la speranza.

But two thieves robbed my treasures:
a pair of pretty eyes.
They came in with you, and all my past
dreams have vanished.
But the theft doesn't upset me,
because it has filled me with hope.

Or che mi conoscete parlate voi. Deh
parlate. Chi siete? Vi piaccia dir?

Now that you know me, it's your turn to
speak. Who are you? Will you tell me?

Andante lento
MIMI

Sì, Mi chia-ma - no   Mi - mi,   ma il mio no - me è Lu-ci - a.

Mimi:
Sì. Mi chiamano Mimì, ma il mio nome è
Lucia.
La storia mia è breve. A tela o e seta
ricamo in casa a fuori. Son tranquilla e
lieta,
ed è mio svago far gigli a rose.
Mi piaccion quelle cose che han sì dolce
malia, che parlano d'amor, di primavere,
che parlano di sogni e di chimere,
quelle cose the han nome poesia . . .
Lei m'intende?

Mimi:
Yes. They call me Mimi, but my real
name is Lucia.
My story is brief. I embroider silk and
satin at home or outside. I'm quiet and
happy, and my pastime is making lilies
and roses.
I love all things that have gentle magic,
that talk of love, of spring, of dreams, and
of fairy tales,
those things called poetry . . .
Do you understand me?

Rodolfo:
Sì.

Rodolfo:
Yes.

Mimi
Mi chiamano Mimì. Il perchè non so.
Sola, mi fo il pranzo da me stessa.
Non vado sempre a messa,
ma prego assai il Signor.
Vivo sola, soletta,
là in una bianca cameretta;

Mimi:
They call me Mimi I don't know why.
I live all by myself and I eat alone.
I don't often go to church,
but I like to pray to God.
I live alone, all alone,
in my tiny white room;

guardo sui tetti e in cielo.
Ma quando vien lo sgelo
Il primo sole è mio,
Il primo bacio dell'aprile è mio!
Il primo sole è mio.

Germoglia in un vaso una rosa,
foglia a foglia l'aspiro.
Così gentil è il profumo d'un fior.
Ma i fior ch'io faccio, ahimè,
i fior ch'io faccio, ahimè non hanno odore.

Altro di me non le saprei narrare.
Sono la sua vicina che la vien fuori d'ora
a importunare.

Schaunard:
Ehi! Rodolfo!

Colline:
Rodolfo!

Marcello:
Olà! Non senti? Lumaca!

Colline:
Poetucolo!

Schaunard:
Accidenti al pigro!

*Rodolfo, impatient, goes to the window to answer his friends.
The moonlight floods the room with light.*

Rodolfo:
Scrivo ancora tre righi avolo.

Mimi:
Chi sono?

Rodolfo:
Amici.

Schaunard:
Sentirai le tue.

I look at the roofs and the sky.
But when spring comes
the sun's first rays are mine.
April's first kiss is mine!
The sun's first rays are mine!

I breathe the perfume of rose blossoms in my vase, I breathe its aroma, petal by petal. So sweet is the flower's perfume. But the flowers I make, alas, the flowers I make, alas, alas, have no scent.

What else can I say?
I'm your neighbor, disturbing you at this importune hour.

Schaunard: *(from below)*
Hey! Rodolfo!

Colline:
Rodolfo!

Marcello:
Hey! Can't you hear? You slow-coach!

Colline:
You scribbler!

Schaunard:
To hell with that lazy one!

Rodolfo:
I've a few more words to write.

Mimi: *(inquiring of Rodolfo)*
Who are they?

Rodolfo:
Friends.

Schaunard:
You'll hear about this.

Marcello:
Che te ne fai li solo?

Marcello:
What are you doing there alone?

Rodolfo:
Non son solo. Siamo in due.
Andate da Momus, tenete il posto.
Ci saremo tosto.

Rodolfo:
I'm not alone. There's two of us.
Go to Momus and get a table.
We'll be there soon.

Marcello, Schaunard e Colline:
Momus, Momus, Momus,
zitti a discreti andiamocene via.
Momus, Momus.
Trovò la poesia.

Marcello, Schaunard and Colline:
Momus, Momus, Momus.
Quietly, discreetly, we're off.
Momus, Momus.
I found poetry at last.

Rodolfo sees Mimi in the moonlight, and he contemplates her ecstatically.

Rodolfo:
O soave fanciulla,
o dolce viso, di mite circonfuso alba
lunar, in te ravviso il sogno ch'io vorrei
sempre sognar!

Rodolfo:
Oh! Gentle young lady,
oh, sweet face bathed in the moonlight.
I see in you the fulfillment of all my
dreams!

Mim:
(Ah, tu sol comandi, amor!)

Mimi:
(Ah! You alone command love!)

Rodolfo:
Fremon già nell'anima le dolcezze
estreme.

Rodolfo:
My soul throbs from your sweet tender-
ness!

Mimi:
(Tu sol comandi, amore!)

Mimi:
(You alone command love!)

Rodolfo:
Fremon nell'anima dolcezze estreme.....
nel bacio freme amor!

Rodolfo:
My soul throbs from your sweet tender-
ness,
the kiss of throbbing love!

Mimi:
(Oh! come dolci scendono le sue lusinghe
al core . . . Tu sol comandi, amor!)

Mimi:
(Oh! How his sweet flattery enters my
heart. You alone command love!)

(Rodolfo kisses Mimi.)
No, per pietà!   No, please!

Rodolfo:
Sei mia!

Rodolfo:
You're mine!

Mimi:
V'aspettan gli amici . . .

Rodolfo:
Già mi mandi via?

Mimi:
Vorrei dir . . . ma non oso.

Rodolfo:
Di'.

Mimi:
Se venissi con voi?

Rodolfo:
Che? Mimi! Sarebbe così dolce restar qui.
C'è freddo fuori.

Mimi:
Vi starò vicina!

Rodolfo:
E ai ritorno?

Mimi:
Curioso!

Rodolfo:
Dammi il braccio, o mia piccina . . .

Mimi:
Obbedisco, signor!

Rodolfo:
Che m'ami . . . di' . . .

Mimi:
Io t'amo.

Rodolfo e Mimi:
Amor! Amor! Amor!

Mimi:
Your friends are waiting.

Rodolfo:
You send me away already?

Mimi:
I want to say....but I dare not...

Rodolfo:
Tell me.

Mimi:
If I come with you?

Rodolfo:
What? Mimi! It would be so fine to stay
here. Outside it's cold.

Mimi:
I'll be near you!

Rodolfo:
And when we come back?

Mimi:
Who knows?

Rodolfo:
Give me your arm, my pretty little one . . .

Mimi:
I obey, sir!

Rodolfo:
Tell me you love me!

Mimi:
I love you.

Rodolfo and Mimi: (*as they depart*)
Love! Love! Love!

ACT II

Evening in the Latin Quarter on Christmas Eve. In the square there is the
Café Momus and shops of all kinds.
Mimi and Rodolfo move about the crowd. Colline is nearby at a millinery stand.
Schaunard is at a stand testing a pipe and horn.

I Venditori:
Aranci, datteri! Caldi i marroni. Ninnoli,
croci. Torroni a caramelle. Fiori alle belle.
Oh! la crostata. Panna montata.
Fringuelli, passeri. Datteri! Trote! Latte di
cocco! Giubbe! Carote!

Hawkers: Oranges, dates! Hot roasted
chestnuts! Crosses, knickknacks! Cookies
and candies! Flowers for the ladies! Pies
for sale with whipped cream! Finches and
larks! Dates! Fresh fish! Coconut milk!
Skirts! Carrots!

La Folla:
Quanta folla! Che chiasso! Stringiti a me,
corriamo. Lisa! Emma!
Date il passo. Emma, quando ti chiamo!
Ancora un altro giro . . .
Pigliam via Mazzarino. Qui mi manca il
respiro! Vedi? Il Caffè è vicino.
Oh! Stupendi gioielli! Son gli occhi assai
più belli! Pericolosi esempi la folla oggi
ci dà! Era meglio ai miei tempi!
Viva la libertà!

The Crowd:
What a crowd! Such noise! Hold tight!
Let's run! Lisa! Emma!
Make way there! Emma. I'm calling you!
Once more around . . .
We'll take Rue Mazarin. I can't breathe
here . . . See? The cafe's right here.
What wonderful jewels! They're like
beautiful eyes! This crowd tonight sets a
dangerous example! Things were better in
my day! Long live freedom!

Al Caffe:
Andiam. Qua, camerier! Presto. Corri.
Vien qua. A me. Birra! Un bicchier!
Vaniglia. Ratafià. Dunque? Presto! Da
ber! Un caffè . . . Presto. Olà . . .

At the Cafe:
Let's go, Here, waiter! Hurry. Run.
Come here. My turn. Beer! A glass!
Vanilla. Liqueur! Well? Hurry. Drinks!
Coffee . . . Quickly. Hey, there . . .

Schaunard:

Falso questo Re! Pipa a corno quant'è?

Schaunard:
(blowing on a horn and producing false notes)
This D is out of tune. How much for the horn and pipe?

Colline:

È un poco usato . . .

Colline:
(at the millinery shop where a woman sews an enormous overcoat for him.)
It's a little worn . . .

Rodolfo:
Andiam.

Rodolfo:
Let's go.

Mimi:
Andiam per la cuffietta?

Mimi:
Are we going to buy the bonnet?

Colline:
Ma è serio e a buon mercato.

Colline:
But it's cheap and dignified.

Rodolfo:
Tienti al mio braccio stretta.

Rodolfo:
Hold tight to my arm.

Mimi:
A te mi stringo.

Mimi:
I'll hold you close.

Mimi and Rodolfo:
Andiam!

Mimi and Rodolfo:
Let's go!
(They go into the millinery shop.)

Marcello:
Io pur mi sento in vena di gridar:
Chi cuol, donnine allegre, un po'
d'amor?

Marcello:
I, too, feel like shouting: which of you
happy girls wants love?

Venditori:
Datteri! Trote! Prugne di Tours!

Hawkers:
Dates! Trout! Plums from Tours!

Marcello:
Facciamo insieme a vendere a
comprar: Io do ad un soldo il
vergine mio cuor.

Marcello:
Let's make a bargain together.
I'll sell my virgin heart for a penny.

Schaunard:
Fra spintoni a gestate accorrendo,
affretta la folla e si diletta nel
provar voglie matte insoddisfatte.

Schaunard:
Pushing and shoving and running, the
crowd hastens to its joys, feeling insane
desires unsatisfied.

Venditori:
Ninnoli! spillette!

Hawkers:
Trinkets! Brooches!

Colline:
Copia rara, anzi unica: la rammatica
Runica.

Colline: *(showing a book)*
A rare find, truly unique: Runic grammar.

Schaunard:
(Uomo onesto!)

Schaunard:
(What an honest fellow!)

Marcello:
A cena!

Marcello:
Let's eat!

Schaunard e Colline:
Rodolfo?

Schaunard and Colline:
And Rodolfo?

Marcello:
Entrò da una modista.

Marcello:
He went into the milliner's.
(Rodolfo and Mimi come out of the shop.)

Rodolfo:
Viene, gli amici aspettano.

Rodolfo:
Come, my friends are waiting.

Mimi:
Mi sta ben questa cuffietta rosa?

Mimi:
How do you like my pink bonnet?

Venditori:
Panna montata! Latte dicocco! Oh! la
crostata! Panna montata!

Hawkers:
Whipped Cream! Coconut milk! Pies!
Whipped cream!

Al Caffé:
Camerier! Un bicchier! Presto.Olà . . .
Ratafia.

Cafe Customers:
Waiter! A glass! Quick. Hey there . . .
Liqueur.

Rodolfo:
Sei bruna e quel color ti dona.

Rodolfo:
You're dark and that color suits you.

Mimi:
Bel vezzo di corallo.

Mimi: *(looking back at the shop)*
That lovely coral necklace.

Rodolfo:
Ho uno zio milionario. Se fa senno il
buon Dio voglio comprarti un vezzo assai
più bel!

Rodolfo:
I've a millionaire uncle. If God acts
wisely, I'll buy you a necklace much more
beautiful.

Monello, Sartine, Studenti:
Ah! ah! ah! ah!

Urchins, Dressmakers, Students:
Ah! Ah! Ah! Ah!

Borghesi::
Facciam coda alla gente! Ragazze, state
attente! Che chiasso! Quanta folla!
Pigliam via Mazzarino! Io soffoco,
partiamo! Vedi il caffè è vicin! Andiam là,
da Momus! Ah!

Townspeople:
Let's follow these people! Girls, watch
out! Such noise! What a crowd! We'll take
the Rue Mazarin! I'm stifling, let's go!
See, the cafe's right here! Let's go there,
to Momus! Ah!

Venditori::
Oh! la crostata! Panna montata! Fiori alle
belle! Ninnoli, datteri, caldi i marron!
Fringuelli, passeri, panna,torron!

Hawkers:
Pies for sale! Whipped cream! Flowers for
the ladies! Knick-Knacks, dates, hot roasted
chestnuts. Finches, larks! Cream cakes!

Rodolfo:
Chi guardi?

Rodolfo:
Whom are you looking at?

Colline:
Odio il profano volgo al par d'Orazio.

Colline:
I hate the vulgar herd as Horace did.

Mimi:
Sei geloso?

Mimi:
Are you jealous?

Rodolfo:
All'uom felice sta il sospetto accanto.

Rodolfo:
The man who's happy must be suspicious too.

Schaunard:
Ed io quando mi sazio vo'abbondanza di
spazio.

Schaunard:
And when I'm stuffing myself I want
plenty of room about me.

Mimi:
Sei felice?

Mimi:
Are you happy?

Marcello:
Vogliamo una cena prelibata.

Marcello: *(to the waiter)*
We want a prize dinner.

Rodolfo:
Ah, sì. Tanto.

Rodolfo:
Oh yes. Very.

Marcello:
Lesto.

Marcello:
Quickly.

Schaunard:
Per molti.

Schaunard:
And bring plenty.

Rodolfo:
E tu?

Rodolfo:
And you?

Mimi:
Sì, tanto.

Mimi:
Very.

Marcello, Schaunard and Colline sit at a table in front of the cafe.

Studenti:
Là, da Momus!

Students:
There, to Momus!

Sartine:
Andiam! Andiam!

Dressmakers:
Let's go! Let's go!

Marcello, Colline, Schaunard:
Lesto.

Marcello, Colline, Schaunard:
Quickly!

Voce di Parpignol:
Ecco i giocattoli di Parpignol!

Voice of Parpignol: *(in the distance)*
Here come the toys of Parpignol!

Rodolfo:
Due posti!

Rodolfo:
Two places.

Colline:
Finalmente, eccoci qui!

Colline:
Here they are at last!

Allegro moderato
RODOLFO

Questa è Mimì, gaia fiorata. Il suo venir comple - ta   la bella compagnia,

Rodolfo:
Questa è Mimì, gaia fiorata.
II suo venir completa la bella compagnia.
Perchè . . . perchè son io il poeta;
essa la poesia.
Dal mio cervel sbocciano i canti, dalle
sue dita sbocciano i fior, dall'anime
esultanti sboccia l'amor.

Rodolfo:
This is Mimì, happy flower-girl.
Her presence completes our beautiful
gathering. Because . . . because I am a
poet; and she is poetry itself.
As verses flow from my brain, the flowers
bloom from her fingers, and from souls
united, love blooms.

Marcello:
Dio che concetti rari!

Marcello:
What rare imagery!

Colline:
Digna est intrari.

Colline:
A rare presentation.

Schaunard:
Ingrediat si necessit.

Schaunard:
She passes inspection.

Colline:
Io non do che un accessit.

Colline:
I grant only one access.

Voce di Parpignol:
Ecco i giocattoli di Parpignol!

Voice of Parpignol: *(closer)*
Here come the toys of Parpignol!

Colline:
Salame . . .

Colline:
Salami . . .

Parpignol arrives in the square, pushing a cart covered with frills and flowers.

Ragazzi e Bambine:
Parpignol! Parpignol! Parpignol! . . .
Ecco Parpignol! Parpignol!
Col carretto tutto fior! Ecco Parpignol!
Voglio la tromba, il cavallin! Il tambur,
tamburel . . . voglio il cannon,
voglio il frustin, dei soldati i drappel.

Boys and Children:
Parpignol! Parpignol! Parpignol!
Here is Parpignol!
With his cart all decked with flowers!
Here is Parpignol! I want the horn, the
toy horse! The drum! The tambourine! I
want the cannon; I want the whip, I want
the soldiers trumpet.

Schaunard:
Cervo arrosto.

Schaunard:
Roast venison.

Marcello:
Un tacchineo.

Marcello:
A turkey.

Schaunard:
Vin del Reno!

Schaunard:
Rhine wine!

Colline:
Vin da tavola!

Colline:
Table wine!

Schaunard:
Aragosta senza crosta!

Schaunard:
Shelled lobster!

Madres:
Ah! che razza di furfanti indemoniati,
che ci venite a fare in questo loco?
A casa, a letto! Via, brutti sguaiati, gli
scappellotti vi parranno poco!
A casa! A letto, razza di furfanti, a letto!

Mothers:
What a bunch of naughty rascals! What
are you doing here now?
Go home to bed, you noisy things. Slaps
will be the least you'll get . . . go home to
bed, you bunch of rascals, to bed!

Un Ragazzo:
Vo' la tromba, il cavallin . . .

A Boy:
I want the horn, the toy horse . . .

Rodolfo:
E tu Mimì, che vuoi?

Rodolfo:
What will you have, Mimi?

Mimi:
La crema.

Mimi:
Some custard.

Schaunard:
E gran sfarzo. C'è una dama.

Schaunard:
The best. A lady's with us.

Ragazzi e Bambine:
Viva Parpignol! Il tambur, tamburel!
Dei soldati il drappel!

Children:
Bravo Parpignol! The drums!
The tambourine! A soldiers trumpet!

(The children run off, following Parpignol.)

Marcello:
Signorina Mimì, che dono raro le ha fatto
il suo Rodolfo?

Marcello:
Tell me, Mimi, what rare gift has Rodolfo
given you?

Mimi:
Una cuffietta a pizzi tutta rosa ricamata.
Coi miei capelli bruni ben si fonde.
Da tanto tempo tal cuffietta è cosa desiata
. . . ed egli ha letto quel che il core
asconde Ora colui che legge dentro a un
core sa l'amore . . . ed è lettore.

Mimi:
An embroidered pink bonnet, all with
lace. It goes well with my dark hair.
I've longed for such a bonnet for months .
. . and he read what was hidden in my
heart. Anyone who can read the heart's
secret knows love . . . he's such a reader.

Schaunard:
Esperto professore.

Schaunard:
He's a professor in the subject.

Colline:
Che ha già diplomi e non son armi prime
le sue rime.

Colline:
With diplomas, and his verses are not
those of a beginner.

Schaunard:
Tanto the sembra ver ciò che egli esprime!

Schaunard:
Everything he says seems so expressive.

Marcello:
O bella età d'inganni e d'utopie!
Si crede, spera, a tutto bello appare.

Marcello:
Oh, sweet age of false utopias!
You hope and believe, and all seems beautiful.

Rodolfo:
La più divina delle poesie è quella, amico,
che c'insegna ad amare!

Rodolfo:
The poem most divine, my friend, is what
teaches us to love!

Mimi:
Amare è dolce ancora più del miele!

Mimi:
Love is sweet, sweeter than honey.

Marcello:
Secondo il palato è miele o fiele!

Marcello: *(hearing Musetta)*
That depends: it's honey or gall!

Mimi:
O Dio, l'ho offeso!

Mimi:
Heavens! I've offended him!

Rodolfo:
E in lutto, o mia Mimì.

Rodolfo:
He's mourning, Mimi!

Schaunard e Colline:
Allegri! e un toast.

Schaunard and Colline:
Cheer up! A toast!

Marcello:
Qua del liquor!

Marcello:
Something to drink!

Tutti:
E via i pensier, alti i bicchier. Beviam.

All:
Away with brooding, let's drink..

Marcello:
Ch'io beva del tossico!

Marcello: *(seeing Musetta enter laughing)*
I'll drink some poison!

Schaunard, Colline e Rodolfo:
Oh! Musetta!

Schaunard, Colline and Rodolfo:
Oh! Musetta!

Marcello:
Essa!

Marcello:
Her!

Le Bottegaie:
To'! Lei! Sì! To'! Lei! Musetta!
Siamo in auge! Che toeletta!

The Shopwomen:
What! Her! Yes! Well! Her! Musetta!
We're in awe. What a dress!

Musetta, accompanied by the old and pompous Alcindoro,
sits at another table in front of the café.

Alcindoro:
Come un facchino correr di qua . . . di là .
. No, no, non ci sta . . .

Alcindoro:
Running like a porter back and forth . . .
No, it's not proper.

Musetta:
Vien, Lulù!

Musetta:
(calling to Alcindoro as if he were a dog)
Here, Lulu!

Alcindoro:
Non ne posso più.

Alcindoro:
I can't take any more.

Musetta:
Vien, Lulù.

Musetta:
Come, Lulu.

Schaunard:
Quel brutto coso mi par che sudi!

Schaunard:
That ugly old fool all in a lather!

Alcindoro:
Come? qui fuori? qui?

Alcindoro:
What? Outside? Here?

Musetta:
Siedi, Lulù.

Musetta:
Sit, Lulu.

Alcindoro:
Tali nomignoli, prego serbateli al te per tu.

Alcindoro:
Those nicknames, please, when we're alone.

Musetta:
Non farmi il Barbablù!

Musetta:
Don't act like Bluebeard!

Colline:
È il vizio contegnoso!

Colline:
He's evil behind that front!

Marcello:
Colla casta Susanna.

Marcello:
With the chaste Susanna.

Mimi:
Essa è pur ben vestita.

Mimi:
But she's beautifully dressed.

Rodolfo:
Gil angeli vanno nudi.

Rodolfo:
Angels go naked.

Mimi:
La conosci? Chi è?

Mimi
You know her? Who is she?

Marcello:
Domandatelo a me. Il suo nome è Musetta cognome "Tentazione"! Per sua vocazione fa la rosa dei venti; gira a muta soventi d'amanti a d'amore . . .
E come la civetta è uccello sanguinario; il suo cibo ordinario è il cuore . . .
mangia il cuore! Per questo io non a te ho più.

Marcello:
Ask me that question. Her first name's Musetta. Her last name's "Temptation." Her occupation is being a leaf in the wind . . . always turning, changing her lovers and her loves . . . Like an owl she's a bird of prey. Her favorite food is the heart . . . she devours them! And so I have no heart.

Musetta:
(Marcello è là . . . mi vide . . . E non mi guarda il vile! Quel Schaunard che ride! Mi fan tutti una bile! Se potessi picchiar, se potessi graffiar! Ma non ho sotto man che questo pellican. Aspetta!)
Ehi! Camerier!

Musetta:
(Marcello's there . . . he saw me . . . but the coward won't look at me. And that Schaunard's laughing! They all make me livid! If I could just hit them, scratch their eyes out! But I've got this old pelican on my hands. Just wait!) Waiter!

Marcello:
Passatemi il ragù.

Marcello: *(hiding his emotion)*
Pass me the stew.

Musetta:
Ehi! Camerier! questo piatto ha una puzza
di rifritto!

Musetta:
Hey! Waiter! This plate smells dirty to
me! *(throwing the plate on the ground)*

Alcindoro:
No, Musetta, zitto, zitto!

Alcindoro:
No, Musetta! Quiet, now!

Musetta:
(Non si volta.)

Musetta:
(He doesn't look.)

Alcindoro:
Zitto. Zitto, Modi. Garbo.

Alcindoro:
Quiet, now. Manners! Please!

Musetta:
(Ah! Non si volta.)

Musetta:
(He won't look.)

Alcindoro:
A chi parli?

Alcindoro:
To whom are you speaking?

Colline:
Questo pollo è un poema!

Colline:
This chicken is a poem!

Musetta:
(Ora lo batto, lo batto!)

Musetta:
(Now I'll hit him, I'll hit him!)

Alcindoro:
Con chi parli?

Alcindoro:
Who are you talking to?

Musetta:
Al cameriere. Non seccar!

Musetta:
To the waiter. Don't be a bore!

Schaunard:
Il vino è prelibato!

Schaunard:
The wine is excellent.

Musetta:
Voglio fare il mio piacere . . .

Musetta:
I want to do my own pleasures!

Alcindoro:
Parla pian!

Alcindoro:
Lower your voice!

Musetta:
Vo' far quel the mi pare!

Musetta:
I'll do as I please!

Alcindoro:
Parla pian, parla pian!

Alcindoro:
Lower your voice!

Musetta:
Non seccar!

Musetta:
Don't be a bore!

Sartine e Studenti:
Guarda, guarda, chi si vede,
proprio lei, Musetta!
Con quel vecchio che balbetta, proprio
lei, Musetta! Ah! ah! ah! ah!

Dressmakers and Students:
Look, look who it is,
Musetta herself!
With that stuttering old man, it's Musetta
herself! Ha! Ha! Ha! Ha!

Musetta:
(Che sia geloso di questa mummia?)

Musetta:
(But could he be jealous of this mummy?)

Alcindoro:
La convenienza . . . il grado . . . la virtù!

Alcindoro:
Decorum . . . my rank . . . my reputation!

Musetta:
(Vediamo se mi resta tanto poter so lui da
farlo cedere.)

Musetta:
(Let's see if I still have enough power
over him to make him give in.)

Schaunard:
La commedia è stupenda!

Schaunard:
The play is stupendous!

Musetta:
Tu non mi guardi.

Musetta: *(looking at Marcello)*
You're not looking at me.

Alcindoro:
Vedi bene the ordino!

Alcindoro:
Can't you see I'm ordering?

Schaunard:
La commedia è stupenda!

Schaunard:
The play is stupendous!

Colline:
Stupenda!

Colline:
Stupendous!

Rodolfo:
Sappi per tuo governo che non darei
perdono in sempiterno.

Rodolfo: *(to Mimi)*
If you would treat me like that I'd never
forgive you.

Schaunard:
Essa all'un parla perchè l'altro intenda.

Schaunard:
She speaks to one for the other to hear.

Mimi:
Io t'amo tanto, e sono tutta tua . . .
Che mi parli di perdono?

Mimi: *(to Rodolfo)*
I love you so, and I'm all yours . . .
Why speak of forgiveness?

Colline:
E l'altro invan crudel finge di non capir,
ma sugge miel.

Colline: *(to Schaunard)*
And the other is cruel and pretends he is
deaf, but he enjoys it all.

Musetta:
Ma il tuo cuore martella.

Musetta:
But your heart's like a hammer.

Alcindoro:
Parla piano.

Alcindoro:
Lower your voice.

Musetta:
Ma il tuo cuore martella.

Musetta:
But your heart's like a hammer.

Alcindoro:
Piano, piano!

Alcindoro:
Lower your voice.

Musetta:
Quando men'vo soletta per la via,
la gente sosta a mira,
e la bellezza mia tutta ricerca in me,
ricerca in me da capo a piè.

Musetta:
When I walk alone through the streets,
the people stop to look
and inspect my beauty, examining me
from head to toe.

Marcello:
Legatemi alla seggiola!

Marcello:
Tie me to the chair!

Alcindoro:
Quella gente che dirà?

Alcindoro:
What will people say?

Musetta:
Ed assaporo allor la bramo sia sottil che
dagli occhi traspira e dai palesi vezzi
intender sa alle occulte beltà.
Così l'effluvio del desio tutta m'aggira.
Felice mi fa, felice me fa.

Musetta:
And then I savor the subtle longing in
their eyes when they guess at my charms
and mysterious beauty.
A rush of desire surrounds me. It makes
me happy, it makes me happy.

Alcindoro:
(Quel canto scurrile mi muove labile!)

Alcindoro:
(This scurrilous song infuriates me!)

Musetta:
E tu che sai, che memori e ti struggi, da me tanto rifuggi? So ben: le angoscie tue non le vuoi dir, ma ti senti morir.

Mimi:
Io vedo ben che quella poveretta tutta invaghita di Marcello ell'è!

Alcindoro:
Quella gente che dirà?

Rodolfo:
Marcello un dì l'amò . . .

Schaunard:
Ah! Marcello cederà!

Rodolfo:
La fraschetta l'abbandonò . . .

Colline:
Chi sa mai quel che avverrà!

Rodolfo:
. . . per poi darsi a miglior vita.

Schaunard:
Trovan dolce a pari illaccio chi tu tende a chi ci dà.

Colline:
Santi numi! in simil briga mai Colline intopperà!

Musetta:
(Ah! Marcello smania... Marcello è vinto!)

Alcindoro:
Parla piano . . . Zitto, zitto!

Mimi:
Quell'infelice mi muove a pietà.

Colline:
Essa è bella, io non son cieco . . .

Musetta:
You must remember that you can't escape from me. I know you won't admit that you're in torment, but it's in vain.

Mimi:
I can tell that the poor girl is head over heels in love with Marcello.

Alcindoro:
What will people say?

Rodolfo:
Marcello loved her once . . .

Schaunard:
Ah! Marcello will give in!

Rodolfo:
The flirt abandoned him . . .

Colline:
Who knows what'll happen!

Rodolfo:
. . . to find a better life.

Schaunard:
The snare is equally sweet to the hunter and the hunted.

Colline:
Gods above! I'd never land myself in such a situation!

Musetta:
(Ah! Marcello's yearning! Marcello is conquered!)

Alcindoro:
Lower your voice! Be quiet!

Mimi:
I feel so sorry for the poor girl.

Colline:
She's lovely, I'm not blind . . .

Mimi
T'amo!

Mimi: *(nestling close to Rodolfo)*
I love you!

Schaunard:
(Quel bravaccioi a momenti cederà!
Stupenda è la commedia! Marcello
cederà.)

Schaunard:
(The braggart is about to yield!
The play is stupendous! Marcello will give
in!)
(to Colline)

Se una tal vaga persona ti trattasse a tu per
tu, la tua scienza brontolona manderesti a
Belzebù.

If such a pretty person stopped and talked
to you, you'd gladly send all your bearish
philosophy to the devil.

Rodolfo:
Mimì! È fiacco amore quel che le offese
vendicar non sa. Spento amor non risorge.

Rodolfo:
Mimì! Love is weak when wrongs are
unavenged. Love, once dead, cannot be revived.

Mimi:
Quel l' infelice mi muove a pietà.
L'amor ingeneroso è tristo amor!
Quell'infelice.....

Mimi:
I feel so sorry for the poor girl. Love is
sad when it's unforgiving.
I feel so sorry.......

Colline:
Ma piaccionmi assai più una pipa a un
testo greco. Essa è bella, non son cieco....

Colline:
I'm much happier with my pipe and a
Greek text. She's beautiful, I'm not blind....

Alcindoro:
Modi, garbo! Zitto, zitto!

Alcindoro:
Mind your manners! Be quiet!

Musetta:
So ben: le angoscie tue non le vuoi dir.
Ah! ma ti senti morir.

Musetta:
I know: you won't admit your torment.
Ah! But you feel like dying!
(to Alcindoro)

Io voglio fare il mio piacere, voglio far quel
the mi par. Non seccar, non seccar, non seccar!

I'll do as I please, I'll do as I like, don't
be a bore, a bore, a bore!

(Or conviene liberarsi del vecchio.)

(Now to get rid of the old man.)
(pretending a pain)

Ahi!

Ouch!

Alcindoro:
Che c'è?

Alcindoro:
What is it?

Musetta:
Qual dolore, qual bruciore!

Musetta:
The pain! The pain!

Alcindoro:
Dove?

Alcindoro:
Where?

Musetta:
Al piè!

Musetta:
My foot!

Marcello:
(Gioventù mia, tu non sei morta, nè di tu
è morto il sovvenir . . .
Se to battessi alla mia porta t'andrebbe il
mio core ad aprir!)

Marcello: *(thinking about Musetta)*
(My youth, you're still alive, your
memory's not dead . . .
If you came to my door, my heart would
go to open it!)

Musetta:
Sciogli! slaccia! rompi! straccia!
Te ne imploro. Laggiù c'è un calzolaio.
Corri presto! ne voglio un altro paio.
Ahi! che fitta, maledetta scarpa stretta!
Or la levo . . . eccola qua. Corri, va, corri!
Presto, va, va!

Musetta: *(to Alcindoro)*
Loosen it! Untie it! Break it! Tear it!
Please! There's a shoemaker nearby. Run
quickly! I want another pair!
Ah, how it pinches, this damn tight shoe!
I'll take it off . . . here it is. Run, go on,
run! Hurry, hurry!

Mimi:
(Io vedo ben: ell'è invaghita di Marcello.)

Mimi:
(I can see she's madly in love with Marcello.)

Rodolfo:
(Io vedo ben: la commedia è stupenda!)

Rodolfo:
(I can see that the play's stupendous!)

Alcindoro:
Imprudente! Quella gente che dirà?
Ma il mio grado! Vuoi ch'io
comprometta? Aspetta! Musetta! Vo'!

Alcindoro:
How unwise! What will people say?
My reputation! Do you want to ruin it?
Wait! Musetta! I'm going!
(He hurries off.)

Colline e Schaunard:
(La commedia è stupenda!)

Colline and Schaunard:
(The play is stupendous!)

Musetta:
Marcello!

Musetta:
Marcello!

Marcello:
Sirena!

Marcello:
Siren!
(They embrace passionately.)

Schaunard:
Siamo all'ultima scena!

Schaunard:
Here's the finale!
(The waiter brings the bill.)

Tutti:
Il conto!

All:
The bill!

Schaunard:
Così presto?

Schaunard:
So soon?

Colline:
Chi l'ha richiesto?

Colline:
Who asked for it?

Schaunard:
Vediam.

Schaunard:
Let's see.

Colline e Rodolfo:
Caro!

Colline and Rodolfo:
It's high!
(Drums are heard approaching.)

Rodolfo, Schaunard, Colline:
Fuori il danaro!

Rodolfo, Schaunard, Colline:
Out with the money!

Schaunard:
Colline, Rodolfo e tu, Marcel?

Schaunard:
Colline, Rodolfo and you, Marcello?

Ragazzi:
La Ritirata!

Children:
The Retreat!

Marcello:
Siamo all'asciutto!

Marcello
We're broke!

Schaunard:
Come?

Schaunard:
What?

Sartini, Studenti:
La Ritirata!

Dressmakers, Students:
The Retreat!

Rodolfo:
Ho trenta soldi in tutto!

Rodolfo:
I've only got thirty sous.

Borghesi:
La Ritirata!

Townspeople:
The Retreat!

Marcello, Schaunard, Colline:
Come? Non ce n'è più?

Marcello, Schaunard, Colline:
What? There's no more money?

Schaunard:
Ma il mio tesoro ov'è?

Schaunard:
Where's my treasure?

Monelli:
S'avvicinan per di qua?

Urchins:
Are they coming this way?

Musetta:
Il mio conto date a me.

Musetta: *(to the waiter)*
Give me my bill.

Sartine, Studenti:
No! Di là!

Dressmakers, Students:
No! That way!

Monelli:
S'avvicinan per di là!

Urchins:
They're coming that way!

Sartine, Studenti:
Vien di qua!

Dressmakers, Students:
They're coming this way!

Monelli:
No! vien di là!

Urchins:
No, that way!

Musetta:
Bene!

Musetta:
Good!

Borghesi, Venditori:
Largo! largo!

Townspeople, Hawkers:
Make way! Make way!

Ragazzi:
Voglio veder! voglio sentir!

Children:
I want to see! I want to hear!

Musetta:
Presto, sommate quello con questo! . . .
Paga il signorche stava qui con me.

Musetta:
Quick, add these two bills together . . .
The gentleman who was with me will pay.

Mamme:
Lisetta, vuoi tacere? Tonio, la vuoi finire?

Mothers:
Lisetta, please be quiet. Tonio, stop that at once!

Fanciulle:
Mamma, voglio vedere! Papà, voglio
sentire!

Girls:
Mamma, I want to see. Papa, I want to
hear.

Rodolfo, Marcello, Schaunard, Colline:
Paga il signor!

Rodolfo, Marcello, Schaunard, Colline:
The gentleman will pay!

Ragazzi:
Vuò veder la Ritirata!

Children:
I want to see the Retreat!

Mamme:
Vuoi tacer, la vuoi finir!

Mothers:
Please be quiet! Stop that at once!

Sartine:
S'avvicinano di qua!

Dressmakers:
They're coming this way!

Borghesi:
S'avvicinano di là!

Townspeople:
They're coming that way!

Borghesi, Studenti, Venditori:
Sì, di qua!

Townspeople, Students, Hawkers:
Yes, this way!

Monelli:
Come sarà arrivata, la seguiremo al passo.

Urchins:
When it comes by, we'll march with it!

Colline, Schaunard, Marcello:
Paga il signor!

Colline, Schaunard, Marcello:
The gentleman will pay!

Musetta:
E dove s'è seduto, ritrovi il mio saluto!

Musetta:
And here, where we sat, he'll find my greetings!

(placing the bill on the chair)

Borghesi:
In quel rulliò to senti la patria maestà.

Townspeople:
That drum-roll expresses our country's glory.

Rodolfo, Colline, Schaunard, Marcello:
E dove s'è seduto, ritrovi il suo saluto!

Rodolfo, Colline, Schaunard, Marcello:
And here, where they say, he'll find greetings!

La Folla:
Largo, largo, eccoli qua!

The Crowd:
Make way, make way, here they come!

Monelli:
Ohè! attenti, eccoli qua!

Uurchins:
Hey! Look out, here they are!

Marcello:
Giunge la Ritirata!

Marcello:
The Retreat is arriving!

La Folla:
In fila!

The Crowd:
All in line!

Colline, Marcello:
Che il vecchio non ci veda fuggir colla sua preda.

Colline, Marcello:
Don't let the old fool see us make off with his prize.

Rodolfo:
Giunge la Ritirata!

Rodolfo:
The Retreat is arriving!

Marcello, Schaunard, Colline:
Quella folla serrata il nascondiglio appresti!

Marcello, Schaunard, Colline:
We'll hide ourselves in the crowd.

La Folla:
Ecco il tambur maggiore, più fiero d'un
antico guerriero! Il tambur maggior!

The Crowd:
Here's the drum-major! Prouder than an
ancient warrior! The drum-major!

**Mimi, Musetta, Rodolfo, Marcello,
Schaunard, Colline:**
Lesti! lesti! lesti!

**Mimi, Musetta, Rodolfo, Marcello,
Schaunard, Colline:**
Hurry! Let's run off?

La Folla:
I Zappatori! i Zappatori, olà!
Ecco il tambur maggior! Pare un general!
La Ritirata è qua! Eccola là! Il bel tambur
maggior! La canna d'or, tutto splendor!
Che guarda, passa, va!

The Crowd:
The Sappers! The Sappers, hooray!
Here's the drum-major! Like a general!
The Retreat is here! Here he is, the handsome
drum-major! The golden baton, all aglitter!
See, he looks at us as he goes past!

Rodolfo, Marcello, Schaunard, Colline:
Viva Musetta! Cuor biricchin! Gloria ed
onor, onor a gloria del Quartier Latin!

Rodolfo, Marcello, Schaunard, Colline:
Brava Musetta! Heart of a rogue! Glory and
honor, glory and honor of the Latin Quarter!

La Folla:
Tutto splendor! Di Francia è il più
bell'uom! Il bel tambur maggior! Eccola
là! Che guarda, passa, va!

The Crowd:
All aglitter! The handsomest man in
France, the drum-major! Here he is!
See, he looks at us as he goes past!

Musetta, with only one shoe, is carried on the shoulders of Marcello and Colline.
All follow the Retreat and disappear.
Alcindoro returns with a new pair of shoes for Musetta. The waiter hands him the bill,
and exasperated, he falls into a chair, bewildered and perplexed.

ACT III

It is February, and snow is everywhere.
It is dawn at the Barriere d'Enfer, the tollgate to the city.

Spazzini:
Ohè, là, le guardie . . . Aprite! Quelli di
Gentilly! Siam gli spazzini. Fiocca la
neve. Ohè, là! Qui s'agghiaccia!

Sweepers:
Hey, there! Guards! Open up! We're the
sweepers from Gentilly. It's snowing.
Hey! We're freezing here!

Undoganiere:
Vengo.

Customs Officer:
I'm coming.

Voci dal Cabaret:
Chi nel ber trovò il piacer nel suo bicchier,
d'una bocca nell'ardor trovò l'amor.

Voices from the Tavern:
Some find pleasure in their cups,
and others in ardent love.

Voce di Musetta:
Ah! Se nel bicchiersta il piacer,
in giovin bocca sta l'amor.

Voice of Musetta:
Ah! Pleasure is in the glass!
Love lies on your lips.

Voci dal Cabaret:
Trallerallè. Eva a Noè.

Voices from the Tavern:
Tra la la la. Eve and Noah.

Voci dal Boulevard:
Hopplà! Hopplà!

Voices from the Highway:
Houp-la! Giddap!

Doganiere:
Son già le lattivendole!

Customs Officer:
Here come the milkmaids!

The gate is opened for milkmaids and peasants with their carts.

Le Lattivendole:
Buon giorno!

Milkmaids:
Good morning!

Le Contadine:
Burro a cacio! Polli ed ova! Voi da the
pane andate? A San Michele. Ci troverem
più tardi? A mezzodì.

Peasant Women:
Butter and cheese! Chickens and eggs!
Which way are you going? To Saint
Michel! Shall we meet later? Yes, at noon.

Mimi enters, and immediately has a fit of coughing.
She then recovers herself, and inquires of the sergerant.

Mimi:
Sa dirmi, scusi, qual è 1;osteria dove un
pittor lavora?

Sergente:
Eccola.

Mimi:
Grazie.

A buona donna, mi fate il favore di
cercarmi il pittore Marcello? Ho da
parlargli. Ho tanta fretta. Ditegli, piano,
che Mimi 1;aspetta.

Sergente:
Ehi, quel paniere!

Doganiere:
Vuoto!

Sergente:
Passi.

Marcello:
Mimi?

Mimi:
Speravo di trovarvi qui.

Marcello:
E ver, Siam qui da un mese di quell'oste
alle spese. Musetta insegna il canto ai
passeggieri. Io pingo quei guerrieri sulla
facciata. È freddo. Entrate.

Mimi:
C'è Rodolfo?

Marcello
Sì.

Mimi:
Non posso entrar. No! No!

Mimi:
Excuse me, where's the tavern where a
painter works?

Sergeant:
There it is.

Mimi:
Thank you.
*(A waitress comes out of the tavern. Mimi
approaches her.)*
Oh, good woman, please . . . be good
enough to find me Marcello, the painter. I
must see him quickly. Tell him softly
Mimi's waiting.

Sergeant: *(to someone coming in)*
Hey! That basket!

Customs Officer:
Empty!

Sergeant:
Let him through.

(Marcello emerges out of the tavern.)
Marcello:
Mimi?

Mimi:
I hoped I'd find you here.

Marcello:
That's right. We've been here a month, at
the host's expense. Musetta teaches the
guests singing. I paint those warriors by
the door there. It's cold. Come inside.

Mimi
Is Rodolfo there?

Marcello:
Yes.

Mimi:
I can't go in. No! No!

Marcello:
Perchè?

Marcello:
Why not?

Mimi:
O buon Marcello, aiuto! Aiuto!

Mimi:
Oh, good Marcello! Help me!

Marcello:
Cos'è avvenuto?

Marcello:
What's happened?

Mimi:
Rodolfo m'ama ea mi fugge.
Rodolfo si strugge per gelosia.
Un passo, un detto, un vezzo, un fior lo
mettono in sospetto.
Onde corucci ed ire.
Talor la notte fingo di dormire e in me te
sento fisso spiarmi i sogni in viso.
Mi grida ad ogni istante: non fai per me,
ti prendi un altro amante, non fai per me.
Ahimè! In lui parla il rovello, lo so; ma
che rispondergli, Marcello?

Mimi:
Rodolfo loves me but flees from me.
Rodolfo struggles with his jealousy.
A chance admission, a step, a word, or a
look arouses his suspicions.
And it starts his anger and rage.
Sometimes at night I pretend to sleep, and
I feel his eyes trying to spy on my dreams.
He shouts at me all the time: "You're not
for me. Find another. You're not for me."
Alas! I know he doesn't really mean it,
but what can I answer, Marcello?

Marcello:
Quando s'è come voi non si vive in
compagnia.

Marcello:
When two people are like you two, they
can't live together.

Mimi:
Dite bene. Lasciarci conviene. Aiutateci,
aiutateci voi.
Noi s'è provato più volte, ma invano.

Mimi:
You're right. We should separate.
Help us, help us.
We've tried again and again, but in vain.

Marcello:
Son lieve a Musetta, ella è lieve a me,
perchè ci amiamo in allegria. Canti a risa,
ecco il fior d'invariabile amor!

Marcello:
I take Musetta lightly, and she behaves
like me. We're both lighthearted. Laughter
and song, the secret of a lasting love.

Mimi:
Dite bene, dite bene. Lasciarci conviene.
Fate voi per il meglio.

Mimi:
You're right, you're right. We should
separate. Do your best for us.

Marcello:
Sta ben. Ora lo sveglio.

Marcello:
All right. I'll wake him up.

Mimi:
Dorme?

Mimi:
Is he sleeping?

Marcello:
E piombato qui un'ora avanti l'alba.
S'assopi sopra una panca. Guardate.

Che tosse!

Mimi:
Da ieri ho l'ossa rotte. Fuggì da me
stanotte dicendomi: è finita. A giorno
sono uscita e me ne venni a questa volta.

Marcello:

Si desta . . . s'alza. Mi cerca. Viene.

Mimi
Ch'ei non mi veda.

Marcello:
Or rincasate, Mimì. Per carità, non fate
scene qua!

Rodolfo:
Marcello. Finalmente. Qui niun ci sente.
Io voglio separarmi da Mimì.

Marcello:
Sei volubil così?

Rodolfo:
Già un'altra volta credetti morto il mio cor.
Ma di quegli occhi azzurri allo splendor
esso è risotto. Ora il tedio l'assale.

Marcello:
E gli vuoi rinnovare il funeral?

Rodolfo:
Per sempre!

Marcello:
He stumbled in here an hour before dawn
and fell asleep on a bench. Look at him . .
.*(Mimi coughs.)*
What a cough!

Mimi:
I've been exhausted since yesterday. He
fled during the night, saying "It's all
over." At dawn I came here to find you,
my friend.

Marcello:
(watching Rodolfo through the window)
He's waking up. He's looking for me . . .
Here he comes.

Mimi:
He mustn't scc mc.

Marcello:
Go home now, Mimi. For God's sake, no
scenes here.

*(Mimi hides behind a tree as Rodolfo
emerges from the tavern.)*

Rodolfo:
Marcello! At last! No one can hear us
here. I want to leave Mimi.

Marcello:
Are you as fickle as that?

Rodolfo:
Once again I thought my heart was dead.
But it revived at the gleam of her blue
eyes. Now it drive me insane.

Marcello:
And you want to renew it again?

Rodolfo:
Forever!

Marcello:
Cambia metro. Dei pazzi è l'amortetro
che lacrime distilla. Se non ride a sfavilla,
l'amore è fiacco a roco.
Tu sei geloso.

Marcello:
Change your ways! Gloomy love is
madness and brews only tears. If it
doesn't laugh and glow, love has no
strength or voice. Are you jealous?

Rodolfo:
Un poco.

Rodolfo:
A little.

Marcello:
Collerico, lunatico, imbevuto di
pregiudizi, noioso, cocciuto!

Marcello:
You're raving mad, a mass of suspicions,
a boor, a mule!

Mimi:
(Or lo fa incollerire! Me poveretta!)

Mimi:
(He'll make him angry. Poor me!)

Rodolfo:
Mimi è una civetta the frascheggia con tutti.
Un moscardino di Viscontino le fa l'occhio
di triglia. Ella sgonnella a scopre la caviglia,
con un far promettente a lusinghier.

Rodolfo:
Mimi's just a coquette flirting with
everyone. A dandy Viscount eyes her with
longing, and she shows him her ankles,
and lures him with promises.

Marcello:
Lo devo dir? Che non mi sembri sincer.

Marcello:
Must I tell you? You aren't being honest.

Rodolfo:
Ebbene, no. Non lo son. Invan, invan
nascondo la mia vera tortura.
Amo Mimi sovra ogni cosa al mondo. Io
l'amo! Ma ho paura. Mimi è tanto
malata! Ogni dì più declina. La povera
piccina è condannata.

Rodolfo:
All right, then. I'm not. I try in vain to
hide what really torments me.
I love Mimi more than the world. I love
her! But I'm afraid . . . Mimi is terribly
ill, weaker every day. The poor little thing
is doomed.

Marcello:
Mimi?

Marcello:
Mimi?

Mimi:
(Che vuol dire?)

Mimi:
(What does he mean?)

Lento triste
RODOLFO

U - na ter-ri-bil tos -se   l'e - sil pet - to   le   scuo   -   te

Rodolfo:
Una terribil tosse l'esil petto le scuote.
Già le smunte gote di sangue ha rosse.

Marcello:
Povera Mimì!

Mimi:
(Ahimè, morire?)

Rodolfo:
La mia stanza è una tana squallida.
Il fuoco è spento. V'entra a l'aggira il
vento di tramontana.
Essa canta a sorride e il rimorso m'assale.
Me cagion del fatale mal che l'uccide.

Marcello:
Che far dunque?

Mimi:
(O mia vita! E finita! Ahimè! morir!)

Rodolfo:
Mimì di serra è fiore. Povertà l'ha
sfiorita, per richiamarla in vita non basta
amore.

Marcello:
Poveretta. Povera Mimì! Povera Mimì!

Rodolfo:
Che! Mimì! Tu qui! M'hai sentito?

Marcello:
Ella dunque ascoltava.

Rodolfo:
Facile alla paura, per nulla io m'arrovello.
Vien là nel tepore.

Mimi:
No, quel tanfo mi soffoca.

Rodolfo:
A horrible coughing racks her fragile chest
Her pale cheeks are flushed.

Marcello:
Poor Mimì!

Mimi: *(overhearing)*
(Am I dying? Alas!)

Rodolfo:
My room's like a cave.
The fire has gone out. The wind and the
winter wind roar through it.
She laughs and sings, and I'm seized with
remorse. I'm the cause of her fatal illness.

Marcello:
What's to be done?

Mimi:
(Oh! My life! It's over! Alas! To die!)

Rodolfo:
Mimì's like a flower lacking water and
sun,
love alone won't bring her back to life.

Marcello:
Poor thing. Poor Mimì!
(Rodolfo hears Mimi's sobs and coughs)

Rodolfo:
What, Mimì? You here! You heard me?

Marcello:
She was listening then.

Rodolfo:
I'm easily frightened, worked up over
nothing. Come inside where it's warm.
(He tries to lead her inside.)

Mimi:
No, the heat would suffocate me.

(Musetta's laughter comes from inside.)

Rodolfo:
Ah! Mimi!

Rodolfo:
Ah, Mimi!

Maarcello:
E Musetta che ride. Con chi ride? Ah la civetta! Imparerai.

Marcello:
That's Musetta laughing. And with whom? The flirt! I'll teach her.
(Marcello runs into the tavern.)

Mimi:
Addio.

Mimi: *(to Rodolfo)*
Goodbye.

Rodolfo:
Che! Vai?

Rodolfo:
What? You're going?

Mimi:
Donde lieta uscì al tuo grido d'amore torna sola Mimi. Al solitario nido ritorna un'altra volta a intesser finti fior.

Mimi:
Where I was happy before your love called me. I'm going back alone to my lonely nest to make false flowers.

Andantino mosso
MIMI

Ad - di - o   sen - za   ran - cor,

Addio senza rancor.
Ascolta, ascolta. Le poche robe aduna che lasciai sparse.
Nel mio cassetto stan chiusi quel cerchietto d'or e il libro di preghiere.
Involgi tutto quanto in un grembiale e manderò il portiere . . .
Bada, sotto il guanciale c'è la cuffietta rosa. Se vuoi ... serbarla a ricordo d'amor.
Addio, senza rancor.

Goodbye . . . no hard feelings.
Listen, listen. Gather up the few things I've left behind.
In the trunk there's the little bracelet and my prayer book.
Wrap them . . . in an apron and I'll send someone for them . . .
Wait! Under the pillow there's my pink bonnet. If you want . . . keep it in memory of our love. Goodbye, no hard feelings.

Rodolfo:
Dunque è proprio finita. Te ne vai, la mia piccina? Addio, sogni d'amor!

Rodolfo:
So it's really over. You're leaving, my little one? Goodbye to our dreams of love.

Mimi:
Addio dolce svegliare alla mattina.

Mimi:
Goodbye to awakening together.

Rodolfo:
Addio sognante vita!

Rodolfo:
Goodbye to my dream of love.

Mimi:
Addio rabuffi a gelosie . . .

Mimi:
Goodbye, doubts and jealousies . . .

Rodolfo:
Che un tuo sorriso acqueta.

Rodolfo:
That one smile of yours could dispel.

Mimi:
Addio sospetti . . .

Mimi:
Goodbye suspicions . . .

Rodolfo:
Baci.

Rodolfo:
Kisses.

Mimi:
Pungenti amarezze . . .

Mimi:
Poignant bitterness . . .

Rodolfo:
Ch'io da vero poeta rimavo con carezze.

Rodolfo:
Like a true poet, I made rhymes with caresses.

Rodolfo e Mimi:
Soli, l'inverno è cosa da morire.

Rodolfo:
To be alone in winter is death!

Mimi:
Soli . . .

Mimi:
Alone . . .

Rodolfo e Mimi:
Mentre a primavera c'è compagno il sol.

Rodolfo and Mimi:
When springtime returns, the sun will be our friend.

Mimi:
C'è compagno il sol.

Mimi:
The sun is our companion.
*(Marcello and Musetta emerge from the
tavern quarrelling.)*

Marcello:
Che facevi? Che dicevi?
Presso il foco a quel signore?

Marcello:
What were you doing and saying to that
man at the fire?

Musetta:
Che vuoi dir? Che vuoi dir?

Musetta:
What do you mean? What do you mean?

Mimi:
Niuno è solo l'april.

Mimi:
Nobody's lonely in April.

Marcello:
Al mio venire hai mutato di colore.

Marcello:
When I came in you blushed suddenly.

Musetta:
Quel signore mi deceva . . . "Ama il balla, signorina?"

Rodolfo:
Si parla coi gigli a le rose.

Mimi:
Esce dai nidi un cinguettio gentile.

Marcello:
Vana, frivola civetta!

Musetta:
Arrossendo io rispondevo: "Ballerei sera a mattina."

Marcello:
Quel discorso asconde mire disoneste.

Musetta:
Voglio piena libertà.

Marcello:
Io t'acconcio per le feste . . .

Rodolfo e Mimi:
Al fiorir di primavera c'è compagno il sol.

Musetta:
Che me canti? Che mi gridi? Che mi canti? All'altar non siamo uniti.

Marcello:
Se ti colgo a invicettire! Bada, sotto il mio cappello non ci stan certi ornamenti.

Musetta:
Io detesto quegli amanti che la fanno da mariti.

Rodolfo e Mimi:
Chiacchieran le fontane, la brezza della sera balsami stende sulle doglie umane.

Musetta:
The man was asking me . . "Do you like dancing, Miss?"

Rodolfo:
One can speak with roses and lilies.

Mimi:
Birds twitter softly in their nests.

Marcello:
Vain, empty-headed flirt!

Musetta:
I blushed and answered: "I could dance day and night!"

Marcello:
That speech conceals infamous desires.

Musetta:
I want complete freedom.

Marcello:
I' ll teach you a thing or two . . .

Rodolfo and Mimi:
When springtime returns, the sun will be our friend.

Musetta:
What do you think you're saying? We're not married at the altar.

Marcello:
If I catch you flirting! Keep in mind, there aren't enough horns under my hat.

Musetta:
I can't stand lovers who act just like they're married.

Rodolfo and Mimi:
The whisper of fountains and the evening breeze heals human pain.

Marcello:
Tu non faccio da zimbello ai novizi
intraprendenti. Vana, frivola civetta! Ve
ne andate? Vi ringrazio, or son ricco
divenuto.

Marcello:
I won't be laughed at by some young
upstart. Vain, empty-headed flirt! You're
leaving? I thank you, I'll be a rich man
then.

Musetta:
Fo all'amor con chi mi piace. Non ti
garba? Fo all'amor con chi mi piace.
Musetta se ne va.

Musetta:
I'll flirt with whom I please. You don't
like it? I'll flirt with whom I please. Musetta
goes her own way.

Marcello e Musetta:
Vi saluto.

Marcello and Musetta:
Goodbye.

Rodolfo e Mimi:
Vuoi che aspettiam la primavera ancor?

Rodolfo and Mimi:
Shall we wait until spring comes again?

Musetta:
Signor, addio vi dico con piacer!

Musetta:
I bid you, sir, farewell with pleasure!

Marcello:
Son servo a me ne vo!

Marcello:
I'm not your servant!

Musetta:
Pittore da bottega!

Musetta: *(leaving)*
You house-painter!

Marcello:
Vipera!

Musetta:
Viper!

Musetta:
Rospo!

Musetta:
Toad!

Marcello:
Strega!

Marcello: *(reentering the tavern)*
Witch!

Mimi:
Sempre tua . . . per la vita.

Mimi:
Always yours . . . all my life.

Rodolfo e Mimi:
Ci lascieremo alla stagion dei fior!

Rodolfo and Mimi:
We'll part when the flowers bloom!

Mimi:
Vorrei che eterno durasse il verno!

Mimi:
I wish that winter would last forever!

Rodolfo e Mimi:
Ci lascierem alla stagion dei fior!

Rodolfo and Mimi:
We'll part when flowers bloom!

ACT IV

The garret: Marcello is once more working at his easel: Rodolfo writes at a table.
Both try to work, but they are uninspired.

Marcello:
In un coupè?

Marcello:
In a coupè?

Rodolfo:
Con pariglia e livree. Mi salutò ridendo.
Tò Musetta le dissie il cuor? "Non batte o
non io sento grazie al velluto che il
copre."

Rodolfo:
With footmen and horses. She greeted me
laughing. I asked her: "Well! How's your
heart? It's not beating or I don't feel it
buried so deep in velvet."

Marcello:
Ci ho gusto davver.

Marcello:
I'm happy to hear that.

Rodolfo:
(Loiola va. Ti rodi e ridi.)

Rodolfo:
(Faker, you're laughing outside but
fretting inside.).

Marcello:
Non batte? Bene. Io pur vidi . . .

Marcello:
Not beating? Well, I also saw . . .

Rodolfo:
Musetta?

Rodolfo:
Musetta?

Marcello:
Mimi.

Marcello:
Mimi.

Rodolfo:
L'hai vista?

Oh guarda!

Rodolfo:
You saw her?
(with pretended indifference)
Really?

Marcello:
Era in carrozza vestita come una regina.

Marcello:
She was in a carriage dressed like a queen.

Rodolfo:
Evviva. Ne son contento.

Rodolfo:
That's fine. I'm delighted.

Marcello:
(Bugiardo. Si strugge d'amor.)

Marcello:
(The liar! Love's consuming him.)

Rodolfo:
Lavoriam.

Rodolfo:
Let's get to work.

Marcello:
Lavoriam.

Marcello:
Yes, to work.
(They start working, but quickly throw down brush and pen.)

Rodolfo:
Che penna infame!

Rodolfo:
This pen is terrible!

Marcello:
Che infame pennello!

Marcello:
So is this brush!

Andantino mosso
RODOLFO

O   Mi - mì   tu   più   non   tor - ni, o   gior - ni   bel - li,

Rodolfo:
(O Mimi, tu piu non torni. O giorni belli, piccole mani, odorosi capelli, collo di neve! Ah! Mimì, mia breve gioventù.)

Rodolfo:
(Oh Mimi, you won't return! Oh lovely days! Those tiny hands, perfumed hair, snowy neck! Ah! Mimi! My short-lived youth.)

Marcello:
(Io non so come sia cthe il mio pennello lavori e impasti colori contro voglia mia. Se pingere mi piace o cielo o terre o inverni o primavere, egli mi traccia due pupille nere e una bocca procace, e n'esce di Musetta il viso ancor.)

Marcello:
(I don't understand how my brush works and mixes colors to spite me. Whether I want to paint earth or sky, spring or winter, the brush outlines two dark eyes with inviting lips, and Musetta's face comes out.)

Rodolfo:
(E tu, cuffietta lieve, the sotto il guancial partendo ascose, tutta sai la nostra felicità, vien sul mio cor, sul mio cor morto, poichè è morto amor.)

Rodolfo:
(And you, little pink bonnet that she hid under the pillow as she left, you know all of our joy. Come to my heart, console my lost love.)

Marcello:
(E n'esce di Musetta il viso tutto vezzi a tutto frode. Musetta intanto gode e il mio cuor vile la chiama ed aspetta.)

Marcello:
(And that lovely face of Musetta is so false. Meanwhile Musetta is happy and my cowardly heart calls her, and waits for her.)

Rodolfo:
Che ora sia?

Rodolfo:
What time is it?

Marcello:
L'ora del pranzo . . . Di ieri.

Marcello:
It's time for dinner . . . Yesterday's dinner.

Rodolfo:
E Schaunard non torna.

Rodolfo:
And Schaunard's not back.
(Schaunard enters and sets four rolls on the table. Colline is with him.)

Schaunard:
Eccoci.

Schaunard:
Here we are.

Rodolfo e Marcello:
Ebbene?

Rodolfo and Marcello:
Well?

Marcello:
Del pan?

Marcello:
Just bread?

Colline:
E un piatto degno di Demostene; un'aringa.

Colline:
A dish worthy of Demosthenes: A herring.

Schaunard:
Salata.

Schaunard:
Salted.

Colline:
Il pranzo è in tavola.

Colline:
Dinner's on the table.
(They sit down.)

Marcello:
Questa è cuccagna da Berlingaccio.

Marcello:
This is like a feast fit for a Caesar.

Schaunard:
Ora to sciampagna mettiamo in ghiaccio.

Schaunard:
(puts the water bottle in Colline's hat)
Now let's put the champagne on ice.

Rodolfo:
Scelga, o Barone, trota o salmone?

Rodolfo:
Which do you choose, Baron, salmon or trout?

Marcello:
Duca, una lingua di pappagallo?

Marcello:
Well, Duke, how about some parrot-tongue?

Schaunard:
Grazie, m'impingua, stasera ho un ballo.

Schaunard:
Thanks, but it's fattening and I must dance this evening.
(Colline rises.)

Rodolfo:
Già sazio?

Colline:
Ho fretta. Il Re m'aspetta.

Marcello:
C'è qualche trama?

Rodolfo, Marcello, Schaunard:
Qualche mister?

Colline:
Il Re mi chiama al minister.

Marcello, Rodolfo, Schaunard:
Bene!

Colline:
Però vedrò . . . Guizot!

Schaunard:
Porgimi il nappo.

Marcello:
Sì, Bevi. Io pappo.

Schaunard:
Mi sia permesso . . . al nobile consesso.

Rodolfo:
Basta.

Marcello:
Fiacco!

Colline:
Che decotto!

Marcello:
Leva il tacco.

Colline:
Dammi il gotto.

Rodolfo:
All finished?

Colline:
I'm in a hurry. The king is waiting for me.

Marcello:
Is there some plot?

Rodolfo, Marcello, Schaunard:
Some mystery?

Colline:
The king has asked me to join his Cabinet.

Marcello, Rodolfo, Schaunard:
Fine!

Colline:
So . . . I'll see Guizot!

Schaunard:
Pass me the goblet.

Marcello:
Here. Drink. I'll eat.

Schaunard:
By the leave . . . of this noble company.

Rodolfo:
Enough!

Marcello:
Idiot!

Colline:
What a concoction!

Marcello:
Stop this nonsense!

Colline:
Give me the goblet!

Schaunard:
M'ispira irresistibile l'estro della
romanza. .

Gli Altri:
No!

Schaunard:
Azione coreografica allora?

Gli Altri:
 Sì.

Schaunard:
La danza con musica vocale!

Colline:
Si sgombrino le sale. Gavotta.

Marcello:
Minuetto.

Rodolfo:
Pavanella.

Schaunard:
Fandango.

Colline:
Propongo la quadriglia.

Rodolfo:
Mano alle dame.

Colline:
Io detto.

Schaunard:
La lera la lera la!

Rodolfo:
Vezzosa damigella . . .

Marcello:
Rispetti la modestia. La prego.

Schaunard:
I'm irresistibly inspired by romantic
expression.

The Others:
No!

Schaunard:
Something choreographic then?

The Others:
Yes.

Schaunard:
Dance with vocal accompaniment!

Colline:
Let the hall be cleared. A gavotte.

Marcello:
Minuet.

Rodolfo:
Pavane.

Schaunard:
Fandango.

Colline:
I propose a quadrille.

Rodolfo:
Take your lady's arm.

Colline:
I'll call the tempo.

Schaunard:
La lera la lera la!

Rodolfo: *(gallantly, to Marcello)*
Lovely maiden . . .

Marcello:
Please, sir, respect my modesty.

Colline:
Balancez.

Colline:
Balancez.

Schaunard:
Prima c'è il Rond.

Schaunard:
The Rondo comes first.

Colline:
No, bestia.

Colline:
No, damn it.

Schaunard:
Che modi da lacchè!

Schaunard:
What boorish manners!

Colline:
Se non erro lei m'oltraggia. Snudi il ferro.

Colline:
You provoke me, I believe. Draw you
sword.

Schaunard:
Pronti. Assaggia. II tuo sangue voglio ber.

Schaunard:
Ready. Lay on. I'll drink your blood.

Colline takes the fire-tongs and Schaunard the poker,
and they act out a   mock sword fight.

Colline:
Un di noi qui si sbudella.

Colline:
One of us will be run through!

Schaunard:
Apprestate una barella.

Schaunard:
Have a stretcher ready!

Colline:
Apprestate un cimiter.

Colline:
And a graveyard too!

Rodolfo e Marcello:
Mentre incalza la tenzone gira a balza
Rigodone.

Rodolfo and Marcello:
While the battle rages, the dancers circle
and leap.
(Musetta enters.)

Marcello:
Musetta!

Marcello:
Musetta!

Musetta:
C'è Mimi .c'è Mimi the mi segue e che sta
male.

Musetta:
Mimi's here, she came with me and she's
ill.

Rodolfo:
Ov'è?

Rodolfo:
Where is she?

Musetta:
Nel far le scale più non si resse.

Musetta:
She couldn't find strength to climb all the stairs.

Rodolfo hastens to Mimi, carries her into the room and places her on the bed.

Rodolfo:
Ah!

Rodolfo:
Ah!

Schaunard:
Noi accostiamo quel lettuccio.

Schaunard:
Let's move the bed closer.

Rodolfo:
Là. Da bere.

Rodolfo:
Here. Something to drink.

Mimi:
Rodolfo.

Mimi:
Rodolfo.

Rodolfo:
Zitta, riposa.

Rodolfo:
Don't speak, rest now.

Mimi:
O mio Rodolfo, mi vuoi qui con te?

Mimi:
Oh my Rodolfo! You want me here with you?

Rodolfo:
Ah, mia Mimi! Sempre, sempre!

Rodolfo:
Ah! My Mimi! Always, always!

Musetta:
Intesi dire che Mimi, fuggita dal
Viscontino, era in fin di vita. Dove stia?
Cerca, cerca . . . la veggo passar per via,
trascinandosi a stento. Mi dice, "Più non
reggo . . . Muioi, to sento . . . Voglio
morir con lui . . . Forse m'aspetta . . ."

Musetta: *(aside, to the others)*
I heard Mimi fled from the Viscount and
was dying. Where was she? I sought her . .
Just now I saw her in the street stumbling
along. She said; "I can't last long. I know
I'm dying . But I want to die with him ...
Perhaps he's waiting for me."

Marcello:
Sst!

Marcello:
Sh!

Mimi:
Mi sento assai meglio.

Mimi:
I feel much better.

Musetta:
"M'accompagni, Musetta?"

Musetta:
"Please take me, Musetta?"

Mimi:
Lascia ch'io guardi intorno. Ah, come si sta
bene qui. Si rinasce, si rinasce . . . Ancor
sento la vita qui. No, tu non mi lasci più.

Mimi:
Let me look around. How wonderful it is
here. I'll recover . . . I will . . . I feel life
here again. You won't ever leave me.

Rodolfo:
Benedetta bocca, te ancor mi parli.

Rodolfo:
Beloved lips, you speak to me again.

Musetta:
Che ci avete in casa?

Musetta:
What is there in the house?

Marcello:
Nulla.

Marcello:
Nothing.

Musetta:
Non caffè? Non vino?

Musetta:
No coffee? No wine?

Marcello:
Nulla. Ah! Miseria.

Marcello:
Nothing. Poverty!

Schaunard:
Fra mezz'ora è morta!

Schaunard:
In a half hour she'll be dead!

Mimi:
Ho tanto freddo. Se avessi un manicotto!
Queste mie mani riscaldare non si potranno mai?

Mimi:
I'm so cold. If I had a muff? When will
these cold hands of mine get warm again?

Rodolfo:
Qui, Nelle mia. Taci. Il parlar ti stanca.

Rodolfo:
Here. In mine. Don't speak. Talking will
tire you out.

Mimi:
Ho un po' di tosse. Ci sono avvezza.
Buon giorno, Marcello, Schaunard,
Colline, buon giorno.
Tutti qui, tutti qui sorridenti a Mimi.

Mimi:
It's just a little cough. I'm used to it.
Good-day, Marcello, Schaunard, Colline,
good day.
All of you are here, smiling at Mimi.

Rodolfo:
Non parlar, non parlar.

Rodolfo:
Don't speak, don't speak.

Mimi:
Parlo pian. Non temere. Marcello date
retta: è assai buona Musetta.

Mimi:
I'll speak softly. Don't fear. Marcello,
believe me Musetta is so good.

Marcello:
Lo so. Lo so.

Marcello: *(holds Musetta's hand)*
I know. I know.

Musetta:
A te, vendi, riporta qualche cordial.
Manda un dottore!

Musetta: *(gives her earrings to Marcello)*
Here. Sell them. Bring back some cordial
and go for a doctor!

Rodoldo:
Riposa.

Rodolfo:
Rest now!

Mimi:
Tu non mi lasci?

Mimi:
You won't leave me?

Rodolfo:
No, no!

Rodolfo:
No! No!

Musetta:
Ascolta! Forse è l'ultima volta che ha espresso un desiderio, poveretta! Pel manicotto io vo. Con to verrò.

Musetta
Listen! Perhaps it's the poor thing's last request. I'll get the muff.
I'm coming with you.

Marcelo:
Sei buona, o mia Musetta.

Marcello:
How good you are, Musetta.
(Marcello and Musetta exit.)

Allegretto moderato e triste
COLLINE

Vecchia zimarra, senti, io resto al pian, tu ascendere il sacro monte or devi. Le mie grazie ricevi.

Colline:
Vecchia zimarra, senti, io resto al pian, tu ascendere il sacro monte or devi.
Le mie grazie recevi. Mai non curvasti il logoro dorso ai ricchi ed ai potenti.
Passar nelle tue tasche come in antri tranquilli filosofi e poeti.
Ora che i giorni lieti fuggir, ti dico addio, fedele amico mio. Addio.

Colline: *(taking off his great coat)*
Listen, my venerable coat, I'm staying behind, but you go on to greater heights.
I thank you. You never bowed your worn back to the rich or powerful.
You held in your pockets poets and philosophers.
Now that those happy times have fled, I bid you farewell, faithful friend. Farewell.

(He puts the coat under his arm, then whispers to Schaunard:)

Schaunard, ognuno per diversa via mettiamo insieme due atti di pietà; io . . . questo! . . . E tu . . . lasciali solilà . . .

Schaunard, each of us can separately accomplish a kind act.
Let's leave the two of them alone.

Schaunard:
Filosofo, ragioni! E ver . . . Vo Via!

Schaunard:
Philosopher, you're right! I'll go.
(They leave.)

Andante calmo
MIMI

Sono and - a - ti? Fingevo di dormire   perchè   volli con te so-la restare.

Mimi:
Sono andati?
Fingevo di dormire perchè volli con to sola restare.
Ho tante cose che ti voglio fire, o una sola ma grande come il mare,
come il mare profonda ed infinita . . .
sei il mio amor . . . e tutta la mia vita.

Rodolfo:
Ah Mimi, mia bella Mimi!

Mimi:
Son bella ancora?

Rodolfo:
Bella come un'aurora.

Mimi:
Hai sbagliato il raffronto. Volevi dir: bella come un tramonto. "Mi chiamano Mimì .
. . il perchè non so."

Rodolfo:
Tornò al nido la rondine e cinguetta.

Mimi:
La mia cuffietta! La mia cuffietta!
Ah! te lo rammenti quando sono entrata la prima volta là?

Rodolfo:
Se lo rammento!

Mimi:
Have they gone?
I pretended to sleep to make them leave us alone.
I've so many things to tell you, or just one that is grand like the sea,
as the sea is infinite and profound . . .
so is my love . . . and all my life.

Rodolfo:
Ah! My beautiful Mimi.

Mimi:
Am I still beautiful?

Rodolfo:
Beautiful as the dawn.

Mimi:
You've mistaken the image: you should have said, beautiful as the sunset. "They call me Mimi . . . but I don't know why."

Rodolfo:
The swallow comes back to her nest to twitter.
(He takes the bonnet and places it over his heart.)

Mimi:
My bonnet! My bonnet!
Ah! Do you remember when I came in here the first time?

Rodolfo:
Do I remember!

Mimi:
Il lume s'era spento.

Mimi:
The light had gone out.

Rodolfo:
Eri tanto turbata.
Poi smarristi la chiave.

Rodolfo:
You were so upset.
Then you lost your key.

Mimi:
E a cercarla tastoni ti sei messo!

Mimi:
And you knelt to hunt for it!

Rodolfo:
E cerca, cerca.

Rodolfo:
I searched and searched.

Mimi:
Mio bel signorino, posso ben dirlo adesso,
lei la trovò assai presto.

Mimi:
My dear sir, you might as well admit it,
you found it and hid it quickly.

Rodolfo:
Aiutavo il destino.

Rodolfo:
I was helping Fate.

Mimi:
Era buio e il mio rossor non si vedeva . . .
"Che gelida manina. Se la lasci riscaldar."
Era buio e la man tu mi prendevi.

Mimi:
It was dark and you couldn't see me blushing.
"How cold your little hand is .Let me warm it for you." It was dark and you took my hand in yours.
(Mimi has another fit of coughing.)

Rodolfo:
Oh Dio! Mimi!

Rodolfo:
Good God! Mimi!
(Schaunard returns.)

Schaunard:
Che avvien?

Schaunard:
What's wrong?

Mimi:
Nulla. Sto bene.

Mimi:
Nothing. I'm fine.

Rodolfo:
Zitta. Per carità.

Rodolfo:
Please . . . don't talk.

Mimi:
 Sì, sì, perdona. Or sarò buona.

Mimi:
Yes, yes forgive me. Now I'll be good.

(Marcello and Musetta return, then Colline.)
Musetta:
Dorme?

Musetta:
Is she sleeping?

Rodolfo:
Riposa.

Rodolfo:
She's resting.

Marcello:
Ho veduto il dottore. Verrà. Gli ho fatto fretta. Ecco il cordial.

Marcello:
I saw the doctor. He's coming. I made him hurry. Here's the cordial.

Mimi:
Chi parla?

Mimi:
Who's speaking?

Musetta:
Io, Musetta.

Musetta: *(handing her the muff)*
Me. Musetta.

Mimi:
O come è bello e morbido! Non più, non più, le mani allividite. Il tepore le abbellirà.
Sei lo che me tu doni?

Mimi:
Oh, how lovely and soft it is. At last, at last, my hands will be warmed and soft.
(to Rodolfo)
Did you do this for me?

Musetta:
Sì.

Musetta:
Yes, he did.

Mimi:
Tu! Spensierato! Grazie. Ma costerà. Piangi? Sto bene. Pianger così perchè? Qui . . . amor . . . sempre con te!
Le mani . . . al caldo . . . e dormire......

Mimi:
You spendthrift! Thank you . . . but the cost . . . You're crying? I'm better. Why are you crying like this? Here . . . beloved . . . with you always! My hands . . . the warmth . . . to sleep........

Rodolfo:
Che ha detto il medico?

Rodolfo:
What did the doctor say?

Marcello:
Verrà.

Marcello:
He's coming.

Musetta:
Madonna benedetta, fate la grazia a questa poveretta che non debba morire.

Qui ci vuole un riparo perché la fiamma sventola.

Così. E che possa guarire. Madonna santa, io sono indegna di perdono, mentre invece Mimì è un angelo del cielo.

Musetta: *(praying)*
Oh blessed Mother, be merciful to this poor child who doesn't deserve to die.
(breaking off, to Marcello)
We need shade here; the candle's flickering.

So. Let her get well, Holy Mother, I know I'm unworthy of forgiveness, but Mimi is an angel come down from heaven.

Rodolfo:
Io spero ancora. Vi pare che sia grave?

Rodolfo:
I still have hope. You think it's serious?

Musetta:
Non credo.

Musetta:
I don't think so.
(Schaunard approaches the bed.)

Schaunard:
Marcello, è spirata.

Schaunard: *(softly to Marcello)*
Marcello, she's dead.

Colline:

Musetta, a voi. Come va?

Colline:
(enters and gives money to Musetta)
Here, Musetta. How is she?

Rodolfo:
Vedi, è tranquilla.

Rodolfo:
You see, she's resting.

(Rodolfo becomes aware of the grave expression of the others.)

Che vuol dire? Quell'andare a venire . . .
Quel guardarmi cosi? . . .

What does this mean? This going back and forth? Why are you looking at me like this?

Marcello:
Coraggio.

Marcello:
Courage.

(Rodolfo runs to the bed.)

Rodolfo:
Mimi! Mimi!

Rodolfo:
Mimi! Mimi!

FINE

END

Made in the USA
Middletown, DE
02 January 2021